PRAISE FOR *THE JOY MODEL*

"Joy is a human condition which God Himself has designed for each of us. As we experience joy, we come to understand how it transcends the ups and downs of life on planet earth and offers peace and assurance in all circumstances. But, getting to a place of lasting joy is a journey which requires balancing being and doing. Here, Jeff Spadafora presents a "joy model" for daily living that can transform us into models of joy. As does the Lord, Jeff wants that for your life."

—Jay Bennett, chairman of the National Christian Foundation

"Filled with practical application and grounded in scripture, *The Joy Model* is a course-altering book on how to discover lasting joy. I will be sharing this book widely with my friends as we follow Jeff's coaching and seek to flourish in our second half."

—Peter Greer, president and CEO of HOPE International and coauthor of *40/40 Vision: Clarifying Your Mission in Midlife*

"Everyone desires joy, but in many cases we struggle to find it or know how to go about living with it. Jeff uses his deep knowledge of scripture along with his incredible coaching skills to develop a model that can easily be followed and understood. For all of us seeking joy in our lives, this is a must read!"

—Dean Niewolny, CEO of The Halftime Institute

"Jeff Spadafora is quite simply the best coach and mentor anyone could hope for. The fact that he has taken time to write a book on peace, purpose and balance—something he both models and coaches—is of untold value to one who applies the wisdom. I recommend Jeff and his book without reservation and challenge anyone to find a better resource on the topic."

—Matt Levy, cofounder and managing director of Credera and founder of Elevate Culture

"*The Joy Model* captivated me. Jeff provides a guide to look at one's "whole life" through his "M.A.S.T.E.R. Plan" sequence which is a very pragmatic roadmap. As I have the opportunity to mentor women in the workplace globally through 4wordwomen.org, *The Joy Model* will be one of those books I recommend often. What Jeff learned from Bob Buford he is passing on to others. Isn't that what life is all about?"

—Diane Paddison, founder and VCEO of 4Word

The

JOY

MODEL

The
JOY
MODEL

A STEP-BY-STEP GUIDE

to Peace, Purpose, and Balance

JEFF
SPADAFORA

Director of the Halftime Institute's Global Coaching Services

NELSON
BOOKS

An Imprint of Thomas Nelson

Published in Nashville, Tennessee, by Nelson Books, an imprint of Thomas Nelson. Nelson Books and Thomas Nelson are registered trademarks of HarperCollins Christian Publishing, Inc.

Published in association with the literary agency of WTA Services, LLC, Franklin, TN.

Some names and identifying details have been changed to protect the privacy of individuals.

Thomas Nelson titles may be purchased in bulk for educational, business, fund-raising, or sales promotional use. For information, please e-mail SpecialMarkets@ThomasNelson.com.

Unless otherwise noted, Scripture quotations are taken from the Holy Bible, New International Version[*], NIV[*]. Copyright © 1973, 1978, 1984, 2011 by Biblica, Inc." Used by permission of Zondervan. All rights reserved worldwide. www.zondervan.com. The "NIV" and "New International Version" are trademarks registered in the United States Patent and Trademark Office by Biblica, Inc."

Scripture quotations marked nlt are from the *Holy Bible*, New Living Translation. © 1996, 2004, 2007, 2013 by Tyndale House Foundation. Used by permission of Tyndale House Publishers, Inc., Carol Stream, Illinois 60188. All rights reserved.

Scripture quotations marked KJV are from the King James Version. Public domain.

Scripture quotations marked THE MESSAGE are from *The Message*. Copyright © by Eugene H. Peterson 1993, 1994, 1995, 1996, 2000, 2001, 2002. Used by permission of Tyndale House Publishers, Inc.

Scripture quotations marked NKJV are from the New King James Version". © 1982 by Thomas Nelson. Used by permission. All rights reserved.

Any Internet addresses, phone numbers, or company or product information printed in this book are offered as a resource and are not intended in any way to be or to imply an endorsement by Thomas Nelson, nor does Thomas Nelson vouch for the existence, content, or services of these sites, phone numbers, companies, or products beyond the life of this book.

ISBN 978-0-7180-8403-5 (eBook)

Library of Congress Cataloging-in-Publication Data

Names: Spadafora, Jeff, 1964- author.
Title: The joy model : a step-by-step guide to a life of contentment,
    purpose, and balance / Jeff Spadafora.
Description: Nashville : Thomas Nelson, 2016.
Identifiers: LCCN 2016004321 | ISBN 9780718083977
Subjects: LCSH: Joy--Religious aspects--Christianity.
Classification: LCC BV4647.J68 S63 2016 | DDC 248.4—dc23 LC record available at
https://lccn.loc.gov/2016004321

Printed in the United States of America

16 17 18 19 20 RRD 10 9 8 7 6 5 4 3 2 1

*To Michelle. Always a step ahead of me in faith.
Patiently encouraging me to catch up. If ever
there was a "glass is half full" person, you're it.
Joy is not second nature to you. It's your first.*

CONTENTS

FOREWORD

Twenty years ago a book called *Halftime* showed up on retail shelves, and every year since then, given how far it's traveled and its impact, I'm more convinced than ever that God wrote it and that my name somehow just appeared on the cover.

In response to demand, one early result of *Halftime* was the creation of the Halftime Institute, a two-day workshop to jump-start a person's journey toward greater meaning and purpose. Two days is only two days, though, and the Institute leaders quickly saw the need to add long-term coaching to the program. A few years later, providentially, Jeff Spadafora came along to take our coaching to a whole new level.

Now Jeff is sharing his wisdom and expertise with the wider world in *The Joy Model*, a roadmap through the landscape he cleared and cultivated in thousands of hours of one-on-one coaching and in leading our global network of coaches. As timeless as Scripture and as fresh as the morning market reports, this treasure of a volume distills twenty years' worth of hard-won truths into a model you can apply to your everyday life. This is rich stuff.

The work to discover your calling, it turns out, is just one important leg on your life journey toward joy. *The Joy Model* maps the full route, providing a fully integrated pathway to deep and lasting joy and to greater peace and freedom, regardless of your age, gender, or income.

After more than a decade with Jeff, I know the depths of his love for God. I've seen the effects of that love—and of God's love for Jeff. And since I know the value of Jeff's company, I also know something of what this book holds in store for every reader. So here is my briefest review: Blessings lie ahead.

—Bob Buford
Author of *Halftime* and founder
of the Halftime Institute

PREFACE

I'm a big fan of Jeff Spadafora. He has been my coach for more than two years, helping me move from success to significance and discover my path to joy, happiness, and purpose.

I'm a latecomer to the Lord. In fact, I didn't think much about Him until *The One Minute Manager* came out in 1982. It was so successful I was having trouble taking credit for it. When people asked me why I thought the book was doing so well, I started saying, "I don't know—God must be involved somehow."

As soon as I started mentioning God, He started sending me people.

Soon I found myself spending time with Rev. Robert Schuller on his *Hour of Power*. He said to me, "Ken, I love your book, *The One Minute Manager*. But do you know who the greatest one-minute Manager of all time was? Jesus of Nazareth." Reverend Schuller went on to explain how, in His leadership, Jesus essentially had practiced all three secrets from the book— goal setting, praising, and reprimanding/redirecting. Until then I had never thought about Jesus as a leader, much less my Savior.

Next, the Lord sent me Bob Buford, and Bob introduced me to Bill Hybels from Willow Creek Community Church. Soon afterward, I was asked to write a book with Norman Vincent Peale. With all of this activity going on, as Norman cleverly phrased it, I finally "suited up for the Lord."

Once I suited up, I focused all my effort on Doing, as Jeff defines it in the book. I cofounded the Lead Like Jesus ministry. I became active in our church and started accepting invitations to speak to Christian groups and at prayer breakfasts all around the country. I cochaired the Luis Palau CityFest, a faith-based celebration in San Diego. I was doing all of these activities while continuing to play a major role in the leadership development company my wife, Margie, and I had cofounded.

After a while, I became exhausted. That's when Margie and I decided to go to the Halftime Institute and see if we could begin to get clear on what the Lord wanted us to do with our lives. There, I met Jeff and was introduced to his Joy Model. When he was assigned as my follow-up coach, I was excited.

With the coaching I've received from Jeff, I've been able to spend more time on the Being aspect of myself—allowing myself to really spend time getting to know the Lord, not just running around trying to practice everything I'd studied from Scripture or learned from my faith buddies. Some people have the opposite problem—they spend too much time on the Being side and don't really venture out into the world to see what they can be Doing to help. The balanced combination of Doing and Being is key in the Joy Model—and achieving that balance has made a big difference in my life.

If you have been overemphasizing either Doing or Being in

your life, and want to find balance and real joy and peace, I highly recommend *The Joy Model*. It will cause you to take a good, hard look at your life, apply what you've learned over the years, and make a difference in the world for the Lord—and for yourself.

—Ken Blanchard
Coauthor, *The New One Minute Manager* and *Lead Like Jesus*

INTRODUCTION

September 11, 2013
10:45 a.m.
The Commodore Hotel, Nashville, Tennessee

I was sitting in a mahogany-lined boardroom of the historic Commodore Hotel in downtown Nashville with nine men who were serious about seeking God's will for their lives. At the time, I was fifteen minutes away from standing up and facilitating a discussion about life purpose. The leader of the retreat was going over the agenda and our plan for the rest of our two days together. As usual, I was 100 percent prepared to lead this dialogue, when all of a sudden—*Bam!* The Holy Spirit started downloading something into my brain, something that had up to that point eluded me.

Here's the back story. Throughout the previous summer, my friend Paul McGinnis and I had been trying to design a simple model to visually explain the concept of joy. Paul is a former coaching client of mine who is now with the Halftime Institute—the nonprofit I am a part of—as a coach and the head of our marketing department. Our shared observation was that the real source behind men and women's desire to know God's purpose for their lives is not altruism or selfless service. The real reason is less lofty—certainly less spiritual—than that. It's a basic human emotion called discontent. There is something going on at a practical and/or spiritual level that is leaving them with the sense that something's not quite right with their lives. They feel a little empty, joyless. That was me in 2005. Some people in this situation assume the root cause of their discontent is that they are not living out their true purpose in life—that they've somehow missed their real calling and have gone down the wrong life and career path. As you read this book, you'll see that they are partly right. But only partly.

Before God spoke to me at the Commodore Hotel, Paul and I had spent hours toying with all sorts of diagrams and models that would simply and visually explain why people—specifically Christians—often feel such discontent. Paul and I wanted a model that would intuitively explain the reason. We also desperately wanted to share how God had moved the two of us from lives of discontent to lives with more joy and fulfillment. No model we ever drew seemed right . . . until that morning of September 11, 2013.

As I stood up to address the group, I did something I never do. I went off script. I shared that I sincerely believed God had been speaking to me that morning and that I wanted to share with them what He had revealed: a diagram that simply depicts the dynamics of true and lasting joy. The dialogue that followed my presentation was rich, insightful, and dynamic. At the end of the two-day retreat, two of the attendees approached me separately and said that learning about the Joy Model was the highlight of the weekend. They finally had a visual road map for improving their lives.

A few weeks later I was co-facilitating another workshop with Bob Buford, author of *Halftime* and founder of the Halftime Institute. The topic of joy surfaced three times during the first morning—that doesn't always happen. I took it as a hint to share the Joy Model. The feedback from Bob and the participants was positive again. During the next break, Bob said, "We need to talk."

At the end of the workshop, Bob and I went into his office to discuss the Joy Model. I shared the background of the model, and he reaffirmed how spot-on he thought it was. In typical Bob fashion, he wanted to press in further: "The model explains where people are relative to joy, but how do they navigate from where they currently are toward greater joy?"

I'd been working on the answer for a while and replied, "It's called the M.A.S.T.E.R. Plan." God had given me the experience of coaching hundreds of people and reading just about everything under the sun (sacred and secular) relative to joy, happiness, and purpose, and it's from that experience that I derived the M.A.S.T.E.R. Plan.

I'm not a psychologist, psychiatrist, therapist, or counselor. I don't have a lot of academic initials after my name. I'm a practitioner. A business guy who decided to follow Jesus late in life and has dedicated a decade of my life to focusing on the practical and spiritual dynamics of joy. The result of this focus is a simple, super-practical process called the M.A.S.T.E.R. Plan that leads people toward lives of greater joy.

After sharing the M.A.S.T.E.R. Plan with Bob, he asked me what I intended to do about all of this. "I've been thinking about writing a book," I said. His reply: "You better believe you're going to write a book, and I'm going to help you do it!"

So here we are. And here you are, presumably on the hunt for a level of joy and fulfillment that has been eluding you. I have shared the Joy Model and the M.A.S.T.E.R. Plan with thousands of people since those early days. The feedback has been nothing but positive. I hope the ideas, tools, stories, and principles of this book make a positive difference in your life too.

ONE

HOW DID I GET HERE?

Buzz. Buzz. Michelle's cell phone vibrated twice on her nightstand. It was a text coming in at 12:40 a.m. I was zonked out and the sound barely registered with me. "Jeff, Jeff, wake up. Look." It was a text from my seventeen-year-old son's ex-girlfriend: "Please check on Neal. He sent me this photo." It was a picture of the palm of a hand holding four pills.

I ran down the hall, flipped on the lights, and tried to shake Neal awake. I could barely rouse him. "Neal, did you take some pills?" No response. "Neal, did you take any pills?" I shouted. In a stupor he mumbled, "I don't . . . I don't know." He was completely out of it.

Michelle came into the room, and I told her to call 911 as I tried to drag him out of bed to get him to the bathroom to force him to throw up. I had to go easy on him because he had just had major shoulder surgery a few weeks prior.

I couldn't believe this was happening. Four hours earlier we had been at the high school homecoming football game. Michelle and I were in the stands strategically positioned to have a line of sight on our two boys (Neal and his fifteen-year-old brother, Quinn) to get a feel for how they were settling into their new high school. Neal, always the life of the party, was making everyone within a three-bleacher radius laugh. "Some things never change," we chuckled.

Or do they? Now, as we waited for the ambulance to arrive, Neal was growing less coherent. Slipping away. And our whole world was turning upside down.

Before I knew it, the paramedics had Neal and Michelle in a speeding ambulance headed for the hospital and I was racing behind them in my truck.

It was a surreal drive. I was confused . . . and mad at myself. How could I have missed the signs? His shoulder surgery was so serious he was going to miss both the golf and basketball seasons—two of his greatest loves. Prior to the surgery he had totaled his car in an accident. He was in a new and completely different school environment trying to make new friends. He and his girlfriend had just broken up.

The week before, he told us he thought he was addicted to the pain meds, and we had immediately flushed everything down the toilet. Now I racked my brain to think of what could possibly be in his system.

And yet, as I drove, underneath it all I had this odd—even inexplicable—sense that he was going to be okay. A week or two earlier a friend of mine had shared how the promise of Romans 8:28 got him through a terrible accident: "In *all* things God works for the good of those who love him, who have been called according to his purpose" (emphasis mine). In the car, I found myself actually believing this verse.

I parked outside the hospital and ran in. The docs had Neal in the emergency room. Soon they came out and told us he was going to be okay. He had ingested a non-life-threatening dosage of the Ambien that I kept in my home office and used when I was traveling internationally. But they categorized his behavior as a suicide attempt and wanted to keep him under surveillance and do some psychological assessments. We could go home for the night . . . a night full of both worry and relief.

We headed back to the hospital early the next morning with lots of questions in our minds, but with huge gratitude in our hearts. Neal was alive. Michelle said something as we walked into the hospital that I'll never forget: "Two things you have to know. First, God has a plan for this. In some crazy way, this is no surprise to Him, and everything is going to be okay. Second, for what it's worth, I don't blame you for any of this." Is there anything else you'd rather hear from your spouse in a situation like this?

So here's the question: How in the world did we get to the point of trusting God so radically? Where did that sense of peace come from? If this had happened to us ten years earlier, we'd have been basket cases.

It might be a stretch to use the word *joyful*, but we were experiencing something in our hearts that was completely incongruent with the horrible circumstances. It was "the peace of God, which surpasses all understanding" (Phil. 4:7 NKJV).

The apostle Paul told the Corinthians: "Praise be to the God and Father of our Lord Jesus Christ, the Father of compassion and the God of all comfort, who comforts us in all our troubles. . . . For just as we share abundantly in the sufferings of Christ, so also our comfort abounds through Christ" (2 Cor. 1:3–5). Over time,

Michelle and I had come to see this truth as our reality and not some abstract theology.

Please don't think I have "arrived" or am some spiritual giant. I still have a long way to go. There are still times when I am frustrated with life. I worry. I lose my patience. I covet things. But underneath it all, I have this pleasant undercurrent of joy. I'd consider myself a 4 out of 5 on the joy scale. Okay, maybe a 3.5. This book is a humble attempt to explain how that happened. How the practical and spiritual parts of my life have unfolded and gotten me to a place of consistent joyful living that I never thought possible.

But this is more than just my story. As a Christian life coach, I'll draw upon the stories of the hundreds of men and women I have had the privilege of coaching over the last ten years. I've come to see clearly the thought patterns, habits, and disciplines that consistently lead to greater joy in a person's life, and I want to share those with you.

JOY DEFINED

Let's start by differentiating *joy* from the term most often used interchangeably (and incorrectly) with joy: *happiness*. Happiness is circumstantial. When things are great at work, in our marriages, in our bank accounts, and with the kids, we are happy. Who wouldn't be?

But when our relationships get rocky, work becomes a drag, our investments tank, or the kids start misbehaving, happiness evaporates. Joy, on the other hand, continues despite the circumstances.

I believe this type of overarching, all-pervading joy is available to each of us, and I want to share the secrets of experiencing it.

At times throughout this book, I'll use *peace, comfort,* and *fulfillment* interchangeably with *joy.* There are certainly some nuances between each of those words and *joy,* but the common thread that I am drawing between all these words is a state of mind and heart that transcends our day-to-day situation. I'm talking about the psychological, emotional, and spiritual state of being that trumps the practical realities of our lives.

At the same time, there *are* some practical aspects of your life that will greatly impact your joy. Now, that might sound contradictory to what I said earlier—that circumstances and situations don't impact true joy. But here's the subtlety you must grasp, and that we'll explore deeply throughout this book: you can improve your circumstances and your levels of joy by taking action on things that are within your control (e.g., your health, relationships, finances, career) and getting them in alignment with God's ways, and subsequently you'll find both your circumstances and your joy will improve. It's about obedience, about applying God's principles to the parts of life you have control over.

As for circumstances that are out of our control (e.g., the death of a loved one, the collapse of a business due to the economy, a diagnosis of cancer . . .), we'll explore how joy can be real and lasting in those situations too.

JESUS

I have been asked many times over the years if true joy is only available to Christians. I can't tell you how much I want to answer that question with a bold and definitive yes or no. The fact of the matter is that I can't. I have studied the world's major religions in detail, but at the end of the day all I have is my personal experience and the experience of other Christians whose lives I have been deeply involved in. All I can do is share the truth of their stories and the Truth that those stories are founded upon.

If you are open to the possibility that the Father, the Son, and the Holy Spirit of the Christian tradition is a possible pathway for real and lasting joy, then read on.

TWO

SMOLDERING DISCONTENT

Smoldering discontent. I can't think of a better phrase to describe my life from age twenty-five to forty. From the outside looking in, I should have been the happiest guy in the world. A beautiful wife, three healthy kids, a successful management consulting career, a dream home in Colorado, three horses to ride on our property and in the adjacent national forest, a ski house in Breckenridge, and a group of close friends. But something was still a little "off."

Your situation may be different from mine, but that gnawing feeling of discontent is probably familiar to you. Something in the back of your mind and deep in your heart that says things aren't quite right with your life. You do your best not to show it, but you know it is there, despite your practiced routines to hide it—or worse yet, to ignore it.

If I were to bump into you as you walked out of church and

ask, "How's it going?" you'd probably say, "Great, how 'bout you?" I might say the same thing.

And we'd both be lying a little. Nothing sinister; not a blatant attempt to deceive each other. But a covering of sorts, which is another way of saying we are putting our best foot forward to try to convince each other—and especially ourselves—that all is well. We are both willing players in a game we have learned without anyone teaching us.

If you're a follower of Jesus Christ, we share a faith that we sincerely want to work; we sing the songs, soak up the sermons, and get emotional over the stories of injustice and abuse and desperation. But something fades when we reenter our work, our marriages, our families—what we sometimes think of as the "real world" as compared to our church world. The real stuff of life can suck the air from our souls or act as "shiny objects" that distract us from our faith and eventually leave us spiritually dry. Either way, we're puzzled about why our faith isn't delivering what it promises us: peace, joy, fulfillment. We wonder if there is some spiritual insight we're missing. Some knowledge, paradigm, or connection with the divine that eludes us and prevents us from experiencing the joy we desire. Or perhaps the problem is more practical: "Maybe I don't have peace and joy because I'm not applying biblical principles to the practical aspects of my life. It's why I have financial stress or anxiety about the path my kids are on or concern about the direction my marriage is heading in." Whatever the reasons, we know that if we don't figure it out soon, this puzzlement could turn into apathy about our faith—or worse yet, our faith will become utterly irrelevant.

Save for the details, our stories are probably similar. You may have been given the gift of faith by godly parents and grandparents—a nurturing environment of Sunday school, mission trips, Bible memorization, and regular opportunities to recommit your life to God. Or like me, you came upon this faith late in life, after discovering that all the worldly things that you pursued and attained did not in the long term deliver what you thought they would. So, like me, you turned to God.

Both of us recall the overwhelming relief that came when we committed to start living life God's way instead of our way. We repented from sin that had separated us from God. We acknowledged Christ's death as the forgiveness of our sins, and we were told His Spirit gave us the power to be free from sin. We were immediately reunited as imperfect people to a perfect God. And we know that the clock on this deal never runs out, even when our physical bodies stop ticking. For a moment, and more, all is right with the world.

Oftentimes, after an experience like this, something fairly typical starts to unfold: the ordinary creeps back in, slowly—almost imperceptibly—smothering our newfound joy with a new type of discontentedness. We soldier on, resigned that this is as good as the spiritual life gets. But, after tasting a bit of joy, we are even more frustrated because it somehow evaporated. *Maybe*, you think, *maybe I just didn't work hard enough to keep it alive. Maybe I've let the cares and worries of this world slip in and move my attention away from God. Maybe the pounding messages of Hollywood, Madison Avenue, and Wall Street have their hooks deeper into me than I thought.*

So we resolve to try harder.

EXHAUSTED FOR JESUS

You read somewhere in the Bible that "faith without works is dead" (James 2:20 NKJV). *Maybe that's the problem*, you think. *My joy is blocked because I'm not doing enough for God and others.* So you went to your pastor and told him you wanted to get more active in the church. Serve God. Use your talents for the kingdom. He told you, "God's timing is perfect." The first-grade boys Sunday school teacher was moving and they needed a replacement. Would you do it? It wasn't what you had in mind, but how could you argue with God's timing? Within three weeks you realized you should have argued—vehemently. It had been nine years since you had a first grader, and even if you did amazing things with your own child, you'd lost your touch. Or kids had gotten crazier.

Serving God looked like this every Sunday morning: Five minutes into the Bible story, chaos reigned. Tommy and Derek started wrestling. Brian wandered over to the toy box and started emptying it. Eric had to go to the bathroom, which prompted two other boys to decide they had to go as well. Only the new kid, whose name you forgot, still sat nicely while you tried to teach him about Shadrach, Meshach, and Abednego.

Maybe in your case it wasn't Sunday school. Maybe it was the elder board, the soup kitchen downtown, the mission trip to Haiti, being church treasurer, or mentoring a kid. All noble acts of "foot washing" service that are essential to developing a humble heart and boosting our gratitude. But long term, it's just volunteering—and tiring. It's certainly not your calling. There's a big difference.

The joy that you thought would come from doing things for

God was replaced with exhaustion, boredom, and perhaps some resentment.

The lightbulb came on during a sermon one Sunday as you recovered from yet another bout of service to the adorable little first graders. The pastor said, "Christians need to go deeper with the Lord. Our faith is a mile wide and an inch deep. You will be continually frustrated with your spiritual journey until you have an abiding relationship with Christ."

How do you do that? He explained, "You need to really get into the Bible. Spend more time in prayer, which includes listening for God's voice, not just asking for things. Get involved in a small group. Fill your mind with the things of God by reading Christian books, listening to Christian music."

SPIRITUALITY ON STEROIDS

After obtaining release from your Sunday school teaching assignment, you got real spiritual. You shifted all your weight from "Doing Things for God" to "Being with God." You decided to buckle down and read the Bible every day for the next sixty days. Each morning you tried to find time to read the Bible for five to ten minutes, said a prayer or two, then dashed off to work. Of course, that commitment didn't hold, and you weren't really reading the Bible every day of the week. Guilt started to creep in. But it was offset by the fact that you were checking some things off your list of spiritual to-dos. As for your prayer life, it was spotty. You tried to do it more often, but you weren't really sure where to go with it or what you were getting out of it.

You heard that being in Christian community was good for your faith, so you joined a really neat group of guys who met for breakfast once a week before work. Wow! Real men, living in the real world. There was a lot of talk about the economy, politics, sports, business, and the sad state of our culture all wrapped in the appropriate Christian worldview. But the focus on the Bible—and the authenticity of the guys—was a little shallow. Not a big deal, though, because you were starting to grow a bit. Call it "winning ugly."

One day your pastor approached you with a new request that made you feel pretty good. He said he had noticed your growing spiritual maturity, adding, "You know, it was probably a mistake to saddle you with those first graders, but our Adult Ed program is growing so fast that we have more people than classes to serve them. Would you be interested in teaching a class of newer Christians?"

If it was hard to argue with God's timing, it was even harder to argue with your own ego.

"I guess I *have* grown a lot," you told yourself. "Maybe this is the sweet spot I've been looking for in my faith."

HUNGRY FOR SOMETHING MORE

So now your pendulum was swinging the other way—from "Being with God" back to "Doing for God"—and you found yourself in front of about two dozen people who voraciously gobbled up everything you served them. You were a big hit and felt pleased with yourself and the situation.

But soon the luster wore off the adult Bible study (or whatever your second foray into kingdom service was). Worse yet, you hit a brick wall on the spiritual side of your faith. Some of the doubts you had on Day One surfaced again, and you couldn't remember the logic and faith that got you over those hurdles the first time.

That hunger for something more reared its ugly head again. That sense that you were missing out. Only this time, it was accompanied by a sort of binary response that scared the daylights out of you: to get whatever it was you hoped your faith would give you, you were going to have to either go all in—maybe quit your job and go to seminary or Africa—or drop out entirely. Maybe dropping out entirely is too strong. But you know what I mean. Just show up on Sunday and return to a more "business as usual" approach to the Christian life. The way things were going with your faith, the gain was not worth the pain. It was tiring. It was time consuming. Maybe that joy talked about in the Bible only happens in heaven . . . or to people more spiritual than you.

It's almost as if this faith thing had ignited a thirst that could never be quenched. Maybe all those unchurched folks who play golf every Sunday morning have figured it out. Here you were struggling with your faith as they happily lived their lives unencumbered by things like church or the Bible or questions about life and death.

THE BOTTOM LINE

As you read this you may be thinking, *Can this guy get any more depressing?*

But ask yourself, and be honest: "Am I satisfied with my faith and life and how I really feel inside? Should I just accept that this is as good as it gets? Do my efforts to serve God feel more like 'staying busy for Jesus' than living joyfully doing what He put me on this planet to do? Why is it that all this spiritual stuff—going to church, reading the Bible, praying, being in a small group—seems hollow and like I'm just going through the motions?"

I wrestled with all these issues from 2001 to 2006. And I know from my work coaching men and women that this smoldering discontent is common in today's churches. But don't take my word for it. Take a closer look at one of the most successful and dynamic churches in America.

THREE

FRUSTRATION REVEALED

Willow Creek Community Church in Barrington, Illinois, is often credited as one of the founding churches of the American "megachurch" movement. Started by Bill Hybels, a youth pastor with a passion for the thousands of people in suburban Chicago who did not know the real Jesus, Willow Creek grew from a handful of people meeting in a rented theater to one of the most dynamic churches in America. On any given weekend, more than twenty thousand suburbanites crowd its sprawling, corporate-like facility to go to church. They've also planted more than one hundred churches globally based on their model. But more than just a feel-good experience, this remarkable church challenges its members to put feet to their faith and provides countless opportunities for them to do so. How many churches do you know that have a full-service garage that offers free repairs to people who cannot afford them (as well as an avenue for its gearhead members to serve)?

Each year members donate thousands of backpacks loaded with school supplies to Chicago's inner-city kids. If you have a skill or a passion to serve and you attend Willow Creek, the church has a place for you.

And yet.

About ten years ago Willow Creek hired a big-time market research guy to survey the congregation. This guy specialized in working with Fortune 500 companies to help them determine if they were effectively meeting the needs of their customers. He had developed unique methods not only to obtain peoples' opinions but to really get inside their heads and learn what motivates them, to discover why they do things. The leadership at Willow Creek wanted to be sure that everything they were doing was helping people grow in their faith. So their marketing consultant went to work with a team of researchers, and after about six months, handed the results off to one of Willow Creek's senior associates.

The results were so bad, the associate was a little nervous about presenting them to Hybels. But of course he had to, and he reluctantly called a meeting with him to go over the survey. Bolstered by the presence of the consultant and a few other staffers who had been part of the project, he waded into the PowerPoint presentation as Hybels listened carefully. The core insight of the study was revealed in the comments from parishioners—more than two thousand comments—mostly along the lines of, "We love this church but feel we may need to leave and find another one that will take our faith to the next level." In other words, "My discontent, which has been smoldering for a while, has reached the point where I need to do something. Like leave."[1]

When he finished hearing the presentation, Hybels responded

as the true leader he is: "Facts are our friends. Let's take a closer look at what's wrong and fix it."

My personal experience over the last decade of helping people discover and live out God's purpose for their lives parallels this research: churches are full of frustrated believers and have very few joyful followers. It's my mission in life to team up with God and others to work on this problem.

If you've been feeling as if your faith is not resulting in the life you thought it would, you're not alone. Willow Creek is but one church, albeit one that appears to be healthy and doing all the right things to engage its members. The most recent data suggests there are approximately six thousand churches in the United States with weekend attendance of one thousand or more. Overall, there are approximately 350,000 churches in America.[2] According to LifeWay Research, an organization affiliated with the Southern Baptist Convention that studies all things Christian, the top two reasons for people leaving one church to join another are (1) "The church was not helping me grow spiritually," and (2) "I did not feel engaged/involved in meaningful work in the church."[3] Sound familiar? You're not the only one stalled on the "Being with God" and "Doing for God" dimensions of faith.

I got stalled on both of those dimensions too.

MY BC DAYS

In many ways, I've lived a charmed life. Born and raised in a picturesque New England town. Great parents who taught me right from wrong and always encouraged me. For whatever reason, I was fortunate to be the guy who not only excelled in the classroom but led all my sports teams at a prestigious prep school. Before I was a Christian, I just considered myself lucky. Looking back, I realize it was all God's blessing. After high school, a scholarship gave me four wonderful years of study and playing football and baseball at Amherst College. Then it was off to a business career as a leadership and executive development consultant in Chicago and later, Colorado.

Talk about the good life. I joined a firm where a few of my college buddies also worked, and after putting in a day at the office, we partied and played to our hearts' content. Weekend ski trips to Colorado. Sports leagues. Barbecues. Hanging out at the local watering holes. Life couldn't have been better, especially once I met Michelle. After we got married, we moved to Colorado (a dream come true) where we raised our three kids surrounded by all the good things any family could want. It was at this stage of life that the smoldering discontent underlying all this American Dream stuff really started to heat up.

When our kids reached a certain age, we thought it would be a good idea to get them involved in a church. With the exception of holidays, visits to my parents' home, and my own wedding, I didn't set foot in a church from age fifteen until I was thirty-five. Although I had been raised in a pretty devout Catholic family, I never had a lot of interest in church. I had this faint notion of God, but I definitely didn't understand or believe in Jesus. He was kind of irrelevant. But I knew that my values of hard work, honesty, and kindness toward others came from my parents, and I assumed they got those from going to church all their lives. I wanted my kids to have those values too, so we shopped around and eventually found a church with solid biblical teaching.

What happened next shocked me. I brought my kids to church to learn good values and I ended up finding out the truth about Jesus. It wasn't long before I accepted Him as my Savior.

As far as I was concerned, this was the missing ingredient in my life. The solution to the discontent problem I was feeling wasn't financial, geographical, vocational, or recreational, as I had earlier presumed. It was spiritual. I guess I always thought of myself as a pretty good guy, not a sinner separated from God in need of a Savior, but hearing the gospel in a way I'd never heard it before really opened my eyes to the condition of my soul. I realized God wanted to do more than just forgive me and let me into heaven. He wanted me to live a rich, fulfilling life here and now. I saw all these references in the Bible to peace and joy and fulfillment, and it dawned on me: "Why am I trying to figure out life on my own when the Bible is the best instruction manual for living the good life?" As a friend of mine likes to say, "It was time to stop paying the Dumb Tax."

When I was a kid, my parents had to drag me to church, but now I couldn't wait for the doors to open every Sunday morning. And I discovered a whole new world of books and other resources that helped me grow in my faith.

I jumped into my newfound faith the same way I careen down a trail on my mountain bike—full tilt!

And yet.

MONOTONOUS PREDICTABILITY

While things were looking up on the spiritual side, the way I lived my day-to-day life—particularly my work life—was really wearing on me. My smoldering discontent, quenched for a while with spiritual water, burst into flames when I took an honest look at my work. Early in my career, chasing a new client and landing the contract gave me a huge thrill. And a nice paycheck, which I'd bank or burn through pretty quickly and then go out and make some more. But now, when I closed a new gig, there was no thrill anymore. All those client dinners; all that travel; all that work to earn the business, followed by more hard work delivering what we promised.

The thrill of winning and making money had given way to a monotonous predictability. Whenever I made a new presentation, I knew one of two things would happen: After the company's leadership team reviewed my proposal, they would call and politely tell me they had decided to pursue other options. Or, more likely, we'd get the deal. Then I'd marshal my team together to design the program and work our tails off to deliver it beyond their expectations. We'd make a lot of money and then what? Do it all over again? Buy more stuff? Take another vacation? I was forty years old, and I had this haunting feeling that this was what my life was going to be like for the next twenty-five years.

And I wasn't just tired and bored. I was actually sickened by the selfish nature of my work. I wanted to make a positive difference in peoples' lives. Leave a legacy. Glorify God. Live with greater joy and purpose. It was becoming clear that my work week was completely out of sync with the formula for joy that I started to see unfold in Scripture.

One day I read a quote by preacher, author, and civil rights leader Harold Thurman that struck a chord: "Don't ask what the world needs. Ask what makes you come alive, and go do it.

Because what the world needs is people who have come alive." That stopped me in my tracks. My faith was slowly blossoming at this stage of life, things were good with Michelle and the kids, but I wasn't *alive*. And it was starting to become clear that making more money wasn't going to do the trick.

My tenth-grade English teacher at the prep school I attended was a big Henry David Thoreau fan. One of the Thoreau quotes that he would subtly warn us with was, "The mass of men lead lives of quiet desperation." At age fifteen, I didn't have a clue what he was talking about. At age forty, I completely got it.

THE WAKE-UP CALL

One spring break Michelle and I took the kids to Disney World. My mom and dad were with us, and we ran into a guy who had played football for my dad. My dad was a high school football coach in Massachusetts for more than thirty years. This former player, ten to twelve years older than I, was with his extended family on vacation too. So there we were, a gaggle of New Englanders all from the same small town unexpectedly bumping into each other and reminiscing. Somehow I found myself shoulder to shoulder with this man who had become quite a successful leader in his life. He told me, "You know, Jeff, hardly a week goes by where I don't call on some wisdom that I learned from your dad on the football field or in the classroom." At that moment I had two emotions surge through me. One, I was proud of my dad and how he had dedicated himself to the lives of thousands of kids in our town. The second was like a dagger to my heart: *If I keep up this life, I'm gonna be rich, but with the exception of Michelle and the kids, I'll probably never have anyone say that about me.*

I knew deep down in my bones that if I put the same amount of energy into helping others and honoring God that I had been putting into making my life cozy, I'd be happier. I didn't know what that meant financially or vocationally, but I was tired of letting fear hold me back.

I had been doing some volunteer coaching for the high school football team on the side, which was fun, but it was all about winning and I couldn't figure out how to weave in the truth about life and God in that public school setting. So I started volunteering at church. I joined the Coffee and Donut Team and the Summer Barbecue Team. I was in charge of setting up the kids' bouncy castle after church on Sundays in the summer. I taught the Bible to middle schoolers. While those were good and noble things to do, the discontent still lurked. I was stumped.

The eager anticipation I had once experienced driving to church on Sunday mornings gradually gave way to a toxic mix of dread and envy. Dread at having to volunteer in roles that didn't excite me and envy of those heading to the golf course or mountain trails. The joy and fulfillment that came when I first turned my life over to Christ was fading, and I longed to find it again. I was a Frustrated Believer clueless about how to be a Joyful Follower.

So it's not just you. And it's not just me. Chances are the person at church sitting in front of you or behind you is experiencing the same lack of joy and fulfillment that you're feeling. So what's the problem? Is our faith just a promise of joy in heaven after we die? Or is it possible to experience that joy now?

It depends.

FOUR

WHAT'S WRONG?

Two songs—an old one and a new one—hint at the dual path that will return us to that place of joy and fulfillment that God desires for us.

The first, an African American spiritual, goes like this:

> *Lord, I want to be a Christian*
> *In my heart, in my heart*
> *Lord, I want to be a Christian*
> *In my heart*[1]

Then there's this age-old hymn from the 1800s:

> *Take my hands, and let them move*
> *At the impulse of Thy love;*
> *Take my feet and let them be*
> *Swift and beautiful for Thee,*

Take my silver and my gold;
Not a mite would I withhold;
Take my intellect, and use
Every power as Thou shalt choose.²

The first song is about our Being: Our hearts. Our relationship with God through Jesus and the Holy Spirit. The second song is about our Doing: Loving people. Serving people. Meaningful work. Stewarding well all that we have. Helping those who are broken, oppressed, starving, lost, and dying—physically and spiritually.

John 15:5 captures the essence of these two dynamics and how they correspond to joy: "I am the vine, you are the branches. He who abides in Me, and I in him [our Being], bears much fruit [our Doing]; for without Me you can do nothing" (NKJV). The Bible calls us not only to "be" Christians through our relationship with Jesus (the Vine), but to "do" Christianity by applying Scripture to all aspects of our lives (the fruit). After Jesus embellished on this point in verses six through ten, He told His disciples (and us): "These things I have spoken to you, that My joy may remain in you, and that your joy may be full" (v. 11 NKJV).

Jesus' two greatest commandments spell it out this way: "'Love the Lord your God with all your heart and with all your soul and with all your mind and with all your strength' [Being]. The second is this: 'Love your neighbor as yourself' [Doing]. There is no commandment greater than these" (Mark 12:30–31).

Take a look at this graph that I call the Joy Model and let me walk you through it step by step. It holds the keys to finding joy in both the circumstances we can and can't control.

THE JOY MODEL

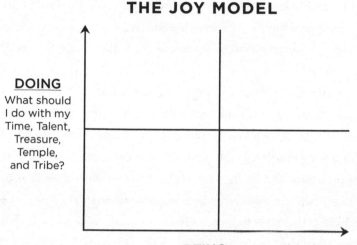

DOING
What should
I do with my
Time, Talent,
Treasure,
Temple,
and Tribe?

BEING
Who is God?
Who am I?

The horizontal axis represents the "Being" of our faith; i.e., the vine—our relationship with and connection to God. Being is *the spiritual process of growing in the knowledge of God and of myself.* This growth answers the questions, "Who is God?" and "Who am I?" Who did God create us to *really* be before other peoples' agendas (both well intended and bad) hijacked our identities?

The vertical axis represents the "Doing" of our faith; i.e., the fruit. Said another way, Doing is *living out all that I am learning and becoming in all aspects of my life.* How I manage my time, my talent, my treasure, my temple (my physical body), and my tribe (relationships with parents, siblings, spouse, children, friends, coworkers, neighbors, and fellow human beings).

This model is a representation of the old adage that "essence begets action." Who we are, how we perceive God, how we see the world, and how we think (our Being) effortlessly flow into how we live (our Doing). The health and nature of our connection to the Vine determines the quality of the fruit—and the level of joy—in our lives.

When Christ followers hit a spiritual, emotional, or psychological plateau—when they are lacking joy—they tend to focus their efforts on one axis or the other to fix the problem. Most people—especially capable and successful people—have a bias toward action and Doing something different with their lives to change their circumstances and improve their level of joy. The problem is that if we focus our efforts on more noble activities but never allow the Holy Spirit to rewire our minds and hearts, we'll never experience lasting joy.

The less explored alternative is to simultaneously apply additional and more creative energy toward the Being axis. Neglecting this path is especially common for people who have been Christians for a long time. They've read the Bible, have some history of prayer, and have participated in other disciplines of the faith. But while they have gained more knowledge and understanding of God, many have determined it's a strategy that has reached its limit as far as improving their level of joy. What's really happening is that they *know a lot about* God, but they have yet to truly *experience* Him. They wrongly conclude that there is no more leverage toward joy to be had on the spiritual/Being axis. They think they've maxed out. They think knowing about God is the same as encountering Him.

When people lose interest in pressing deeper into knowing God, it's usually because they feel they have sufficient theological information about Him. "What more is there to know?" they might say. Again, what they don't realize is that there is a difference between knowing about God and really knowing Him personally. You know *about* the president of the United States, but you truly *know* your best friend. It's a real game changer when someone moves from knowing about God to experiencing His love and grace.

Another reason why some believers who have plateaued in life don't lean into the Being question is because they think they already have a full answer to the "Who am I?" question. They've done the assessments, the spiritual gifts survey, and a bunch of the occupational and psychological profiles, but the answer about what to do with their life didn't magically appear. They got frustrated because they couldn't move from insight to action. My experience also suggests that most people wrongly think these tools have provided a full answer to "Who am I?" They may know something about their skills and personality, but most people are blind to their fears, paralyzed by their assumed constraints, and bound by limiting thinking patterns. The default path is "I might as well just get busy and start doing a bunch of stuff to try to hustle my way out of my funk and toward joy and purpose. After all," they say, "even a blind squirrel finds a nut now and then."

(Please note that in chapter 7, we'll dig into why most peoples' awareness of who they really are is actually quite shallow. The good news is that going deeper into who you really are is simple. Not easy. But simple.)

The challenge in all of this is to be more creative about how to break through our Being plateaus at the same time we proactively make bold changes in the Doing parts of our lives.

WHERE AM I?

When I accepted Christ as my Savior, I moved onto the Joy Model in the lower-left-hand quadrant. I was going to heaven through God's grace: "For God so loved the world that he gave his one and only Son, that whoever believes in him shall not perish but have eternal life" (John 3:16). I initially laser beamed my energy on the Being axis, especially the "Who is God?" question. I was so new to it all. I started reading the Bible as though my life depended on it—and spiritually speaking, it did. I also started reading John Eldredge, Dallas Willard, A. W. Tozer, Myles Munroe, Henri Nouwen, C. S. Lewis, John Ortberg, and Richard Foster. I knew that I was a rookie, and I wanted to enjoy the same spiritual maturity I saw in the "saints" of the church.

You've seen them. Every church has at least one—fortunate churches have many—and they form the backbone of spirituality in their respective congregations. The woman who has memorized huge portions of Scripture and just when you seem to need it most, shares the perfect wisdom from God with you. Or the guy who is filled with such spiritual depth that even the pastor goes to him for advice. Or my friend who is suffering with cancer who fills the chemo clinic with laughter, fun, and enthusiasm that we all know is from God. Doctors and nurses look forward to his visits because of his spirit. He prays with other cancer patients, gives encouragement to family members. His cancer might be incurable, yet his faith is so strong and his relationship with God so real that others are drawn to him.

That's the kind of Christian we all want to be. But ultimately, my approach to spiritual growth stopped after a few years. I stalled—I thought my *knowledge about God* was tapped out, but I wasn't *experiencing* Him. At that point in time, I didn't even know there was a difference. And I didn't know anyone willing or able to help me. Based on the Joy Model, I was stalled in the lower-left-hand quadrant as a Frustrated Believer.

THE JOY MODEL

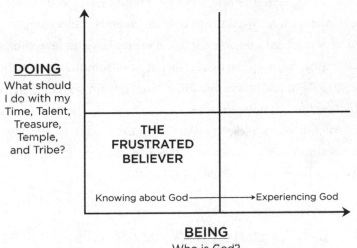

I've learned from my coaching experience that there are a few reasons for spiritual growth plateaus like this:

1. People don't know there is another level of spiritual growth and joy available to them.
2. They don't proactively seek someone more spiritually mature to coach and disciple them.

A third reason, however, is most common:

3. The busyness of life limits our time in the Word, on our knees, and in our efforts to intentionally grow.

Instead of truly studying and meditating on the Bible, we read a few verses, say a quick prayer, and check it off the list without really expecting to hear from God or to be changed in some fundamental way. We don't pray often enough, and we've never seriously explored how to pray. We don't understand how things like fasting, worship, sacrificial service, and solitude fit into the picture. We know a little bit about God, but we certainly aren't experiencing His holy presence.

All too often these tried-and-true disciplines of the faith devolve into obligations—another box to check on my to-do list rather than real nourishment for my soul.

SHIFTING GEARS

When the search for joy on the Being path appears to be a dead end, people naturally start applying energy to the Doing path to relieve their discontent. That's what I did when my faith began to sputter. I sensed my spiritual plateau was actually the result of disobedience, selfishness, and a lack of serving others, so I started working toward the upper-left-hand quadrant. I shifted into performance mode, hoping that would earn me the joy God promises us.

I've seen lots of people work hard to get themselves into that upper-left-hand quadrant. They are motivated by guilt and shame, not love and gratitude. They serve more. Try to sin less. Try to be better husbands, wives, parents, friends, and givers. To be honest, we need more Christians who are intentional and sacrificial about becoming better people in our world. But loving others without the Holy Spirit supernaturally powering us is not sustainable. These folks don't have much of an appetite to move to the right on the Being axis because they don't see any more value to be gained. They just focus on doing more good Christian works and end up stuck in the upper-left-hand quadrant. Anyone who is trapped here for a long time becomes angry and exhausted. They just become Weary Workers. It happens to the best of us when we're operating under our own steam and we're disconnected from the Vine for too long.

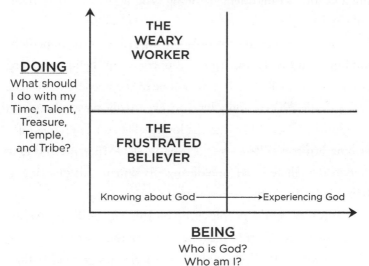

THE JOY MODEL

DOING
What should I do with my Time, Talent, Treasure, Temple, and Tribe?

THE WEARY WORKER

THE FRUSTRATED BELIEVER

Knowing about God——→Experiencing God

BEING
Who is God?
Who am I?

Even Mother Teresa, Nobel Prize–winning missionary to Calcutta, suffered from Weary Worker syndrome. In *Come Be*

My Light, private letters revealed that she ceased to feel God's presence shortly after beginning her ministry in Calcutta. She worried her work *for* Jesus was getting in the way of her relationship *with* Jesus.[3]

Sure, faith without works is dead, as the apostle James warned, but works without faith can be just as lifeless. For many, it becomes essentially a lifelong quest to earn their salvation and God's love, which of course we cannot do. "If I serve a few more meals to the homeless or am nicer to my wife or give more financially. If I just try harder, my faith will come alive and I'll experience the joy and fulfillment that is missing from my life." Without the Spirit of God replenishing us, it'll never work.

People get lured into this quadrant because Doing is visible, tangible, and action-oriented. Being is soft, passive, mysterious, and confusing.

One painful result of people getting stuck in the upper-left-hand quadrant is not just spiritual dryness, but being sentenced to a life of mere volunteering with none of the freedom that a true calling brings. These folks tend to eventually have a big crash and plummet back down into the lower-left-hand quadrant. They become Frustrated Believers all over again. If they pretend long enough that there is no smoldering discontent still gnawing at them, their denial slips into spiritual apathy.

Part of the reason people camp on this side of the Joy Model for so long is because they mistakenly think the "eternal life" spoken of in John 3:16 applies only to a heaven they go to after their hearts stop ticking. They think life on earth is misery—pick up your cross, suffer for Jesus, bear your burdens. Some resort to a mentality where they just can't wait to die and "go be with

Jesus." It's kind of morbid, really. And certainly bad theology. They somehow miss the definition of "eternal life" that Jesus gave us just fourteen chapters later: "Now this is eternal life: that they know you, the only true God, and Jesus Christ, whom you have sent" (John 17:3). We don't have to die to do that. Heaven on earth is literally available to us right now! There is a whole other level of joy that exists that people aren't aware of.

DELUSION

Getting stuck in the lower-right-hand quadrant is hardly any better. It's where people have lots of energy for more spiritual activities, but their hearts aren't changing. And nothing about the day-to-day way they live their lives changes either. For people here, there is no love in action on the Doing side of life.

When I first showed this model to my pastor, he came up with a couple of labels for these folks: "Spiritual Gluttons" and "Bible Junkies." Unlike people in the upper-left-hand quadrant who burn out and plummet, people in the lower-right-hand quadrant can stay there for years. Even their whole lives. The truth is, they're not really experiencing God and growing into full awareness of who God created them to be. If they were, they would naturally and joyfully flow into the upper-right-hand quadrant. When you truly experience God—live fully in His presence— you will become more loving, more joyful, and will be gripped with an irresistible desire to share that love and joy. Short of that, we look spiritual on the outside, but the lack of love in our hearts tells the real story. We become Heartless Hypocrites.

THE JOY MODEL

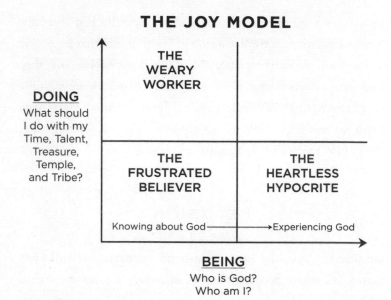

Another reason people get stuck here is because as we travel the pathway toward knowing God we're forced to take an honest look at ourselves: our character, our integrity, our fears, our shame, our guilt. Certain truths about our hearts are revealed that we'd prefer to hide or ignore. We start to recognize fears, greed, pride, laziness, lies, and shame that we'd rather not deal with. Some call this "The Shadow Self" or "The False Self," and we must all wrestle with it at some time or another if we're ever going to break through to joy. We'll only grow if we're willing to get fully honest and vulnerable.

But I can't be too hard on people stuck in the lower-right-hand quadrant. They may be sincerely trying to experience God. They just don't know how to do it. Dutifully they go through the disciplines of the Christian life, but sadly they are stuck with stale rituals.

They may be trying to understand and live out of their real

selves, but the fear and pain of doing that is too hard to deal with, so they stay tied to the comfortable, yet sub-optimized, false self.

The goal, of course, is to break through to the upper-right-hand quadrant. It is here that you will experience the joy, peace, and fulfillment you have expected from your faith all along. It is where God will produce great fruit and kingdom impact *through* you. But He'll also be producing great fruit *in* you. It's the spiritual fruit spoken of in Galatians 5:22–23: peace, love, joy, patience, kindness, gentleness, faithfulness, goodness, and self-control. This spiritual fruit is a supernatural new disposition—even a new personality. It flourishes regardless of the practical and circumstantial aspects of our lives.

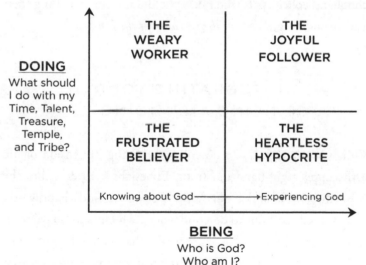

THE JOY MODEL

	THE WEARY WORKER	THE JOYFUL FOLLOWER
DOING What should I do with my Time, Talent, Treasure, Temple, and Tribe?	THE FRUSTRATED BELIEVER	THE HEARTLESS HYPOCRITE

Knowing about God ⟶ Experiencing God

BEING
Who is God?
Who am I?

I spoke with a former construction executive and real estate developer who worked for a year with a Christian coach on both his Being and his Doing. I asked him if there was anything observably different as a result of that coaching—anything his friends could actually see in his life. He said, "Yeah. People tell me I walk slower now. I used to be so high octane, frantic, over-scheduled, and frazzled. And without me even knowing it, I walk slower now." The spirit and peace that come from really knowing God had transformed him. He knows his gifts and his fears, and he's 100 percent confident about where to focus his time and energy. He's no longer living a "Whack-a Mole" life. He's focused, calm, and sees the big sovereign picture of God's plan. That's the supernatural spiritual fruit of joy and patience, and it causes him to walk slowly with peace in his heart.

The same transformation happened to me. I am sure my high school and college pals who knew the BC me are scratching their heads wondering, *What in the world happened to Spad?*

INTEGRATING YOUR
BEING AND DOING

While Galatians 5:22–23 describes the Being dimension of life in the upper-right-hand quadrant, Ephesians 2:10 describes the Doing dimension of that quadrant: "For we are God's handiwork, created in Christ Jesus to do good works, which God prepared in advance for us to do." These are works that we are free to do or not do. It's up to us to step into them if we so choose. It's that wonderful balance between free will and trusting that the teachings of Jesus—as counterintuitive and countercultural as they may seem—really are the pathway to joy.

THE JOY MODEL

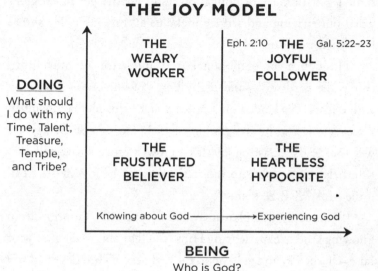

Notice, too, that "works" is plural. Works doesn't only refer to our calling or purpose or mission. Thinking solely in those terms is too narrow. It's about applying all we are learning about God—and who He is shaping us to be—to every part of our lives: our time, talents, treasures, temple, and tribe.

Bob Buford contends that when we stand before God at the moment of death, we will be asked two questions: (1) "What did you do about the Jesus question?" (Being), and (2) "What did you do with what I gave you to work with?" (Doing). The yearning in our hearts not only to be Christians but to do Christianity in a way that honors Jesus is a good thing because ultimately we will be held accountable for both. But like all good things, we need to learn how to manage this yearning so that it produces the joy and fulfillment God wants for us instead of becoming some legalistic duty or obligation. God doesn't get much glory when our striving and service make us all miserable. He shines best when we shine.

Through a lot of personal trial and error—I often learn things the hard way—and many hours of one-on-one coaching with clients, I've landed on a process that helps men and women discover the healthy integration of their Doing and Being in a way that leads to lasting joy. It's a growth process that will over time help you navigate up and to the right in the Joy Model. I call it the M.A.S.T.E.R. Plan.

If you apply this plan to your life, you will transition from knowing God to experiencing Him. You'll be able to identify your false self, shed it, and grab on to the real person God designed you to be. And then, gradually and willingly, you'll start living all the practical parts of your life in an easy, effortless, integrated, and authentic way. Now that's joy!

Four points of caution before we dive further into the M.A.S.T.E.R. Plan.

1. Learning about the M.A.S.T.E.R. Plan may lead you to think this is some paint-by-numbers formula. The journey toward joy is more mysterious than any formula. At the same time, I know from experience that people need intuitive mental models to let the Spirit guide them.

2. Seeking joy for joy's sake is like chasing a butterfly. The harder you pursue it, the more elusive it becomes. Joy, peace, and fulfillment will always elude you if they are your focal point or "end game." It's best to focus on knowing God, experiencing God, glorifying God, and living

the practical parts of your life in obedience to God. Joy, peace, and fulfillment are by-products of that focus.

3. Many people say Christianity is not about trying harder. That it's all about grace and unmerited favor and not legalism or performance. I agree . . . sort of. Grace is indeed a free gift, but like a Christmas gift under the tree, you'll need to get off the couch, pick it up, unwrap it, read the manual, and do something with it. Sacrifice, discomfort, discipline, and courage are huge factors in building a life of greater joy. If you want your life to change, you'll have to change some things about your life.

4. This journey to joy and fulfillment will take some time. In our microwave culture, speed is king. But when it comes to joy and deep inner peace, you won't get there with a quick technique or a magic pill. Nor will you find it by making a giant, bet-the-farm, change-my-life decision. It's more like a hundred small, obedient, and courageous decisions over time. Joy and peace don't often show up in an epiphany or a burning-bush experience. It's more like growing corn than popping it.

With that said, here are the components of the M.A.S.T.E.R. Plan:

- **M**argin
- **A**biding
- **S**elf-awareness
- **T**reasure and Temple
- **E**ngagement
- **R**elationships

In the remainder of this book, we will take a closer look at these six components and how they interact over time to produce a joyful and fruitful life that lasts for the long haul. Margin is, without a doubt, the first step. We have to create some margin in our calendars (easier said than done) before we can find the time to lean into any of the other aspects of our lives.

Abiding and self-awareness are parallel. Abiding with God—that is, really getting to know Him—goes hand in hand with getting to know yourself. As you start understanding and experiencing the Spirit of God and as you begin to understand your strengths, passions, fears, energy drainers, false beliefs, self-deceptions, and limiting thinking, you'll know where your energy needs to go next: Do you need to look at your finances to free yourself from the fears and stress associated with your *treasure*? Do you truly see your physical body as the *temple* where the Holy Spirit resides and flows out into the world in the form of love? Maybe it's time to simply step up and boldly *engage* in issues and causes that interest you. Or you may realize your best next step toward joy is to pay attention to the broken and undernourished *relationships* in your life—i.e., your *tribe*: your parents, siblings, spouse, children, friends, neighbors, coworkers, and fellow human beings. All of these elements have a huge impact on our joy. As you might imagine, the process is not so linear as the M.A.S.T.E.R. acrostic suggests. It's circular, organic, and ever-evolving.

Think of it this way:

One of the tricks to this adventure called life is to make the journey as enjoyable as you imagine the destination will be. So have fun and start moving forward.

Is there enough room in your life for that to happen?

THE MASTER PLAN SEQUENCE

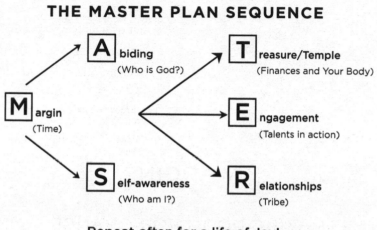

M argin
(Time)

A biding
(Who is God?)

S elf-awareness
(Who am I?)

T reasure/Temple
(Finances and Your Body)

E ngagement
(Talents in action)

R elationships
(Tribe)

Repeat often for a life of Joy!

MARGIN

MAKING ROOM FOR CHANGE

Life shouldn't be so busy. Futurists back in the 1950s and '60s predicted that by the end of the twentieth century, people would be working an average of twenty-four hours a week. Our biggest challenge entering the twenty-first century would be how we would spend all that extra leisure time. Computers and other technological innovations would free us up from menial labor, developing unprecedented opportunities for rest and recreation.

How's that working for you?

According to a Lou Harris poll, not so good. Our leisure time has shrunk by 37 percent since 1973. And the average work week has stretched from forty-one hours to forty-seven hours.[1] For professionals today, it is not uncommon to log seventy- to eighty-hour workweeks. This is one reason why the initial peace and joy I experienced in my newfound faith started to fade. I was so busy that I had no time to dedicate toward genuine spiritual growth on the Being axis or thoughtfully analyze my life and make practical changes on the Doing axis. I was living the classic hamster wheel life.

My personal experience on the treadmill leads me to tell all my clients, "No margin. No mission." You won't experience purpose, meaning, and joy if you don't create margin in your calendar to proactively make changes in your life. And creating margin is hard work. We won't push through the effort to create that margin until one of two things happens:

1. The discomfort of the status quo of our lives becomes so painful that we are compelled to finally take action, or
2. We have a clear vision of what a better life could look like and we're so drawn to it that we'll break down walls to get there.

Without either of these, we'll be stuck. We'll swirl endlessly in the frustration of the status quo while busyness, lack of fulfillment, and lack of vision define our lives.

As creatures of comfort, most of us tolerate the low-grade discontent of a lukewarm life that's "okay, but not great." We go through the motions, content with the assurance, perhaps, that we're on our way to heaven and that maybe a life of joy, adventure, and rich relationships is just a little too unrealistic. We'll most likely fail at any significant life-change endeavor if we don't get to the point where we're frustrated enough to admit, "I can't do this anymore, and I don't know how to figure it out." Too often, sadly, it takes more than a gentle whisper to prompt us to get serious about making big changes in our lives. It takes brokenness. Failure in our careers. Divorce. A nasty health report that includes the *C* word. The death of someone close to us. Many of the people I have coached lived with smoldering discontent for a long time until something finally broke. The pain ultimately compelled them to seek relief and gave them the courage, drive, and discipline to make the tough choices in their lives and start changing things.

Not all reach the point of real commitment to change via catastrophe, however. I'm a case in point. Many people reach this turning point after having what I call a "King Solomon Experience." The Bible says that King Solomon was the richest and wisest man to have ever lived (2 Chron. 9:22). Some economic historians calculate that in terms of a percentage of the world's total wealth, King Solomon was wealthier than John D. Rockefeller and Andrew Carnegie combined. (For the curious, Bill Gates and Warren Buffet don't make the Top 10 All-Time list.)[2] In the book of Ecclesiastes, King Solomon said that his constant pursuit of wealth, power, knowledge, travel, and carnal experiences were, in the end, nothing but "a chasing after the wind" (1:14). He reached the point of real commitment to real change as a result of experiencing the emptiness of success, not the sting of catastrophe. It's silly to mention my name in the same breath as these others because I never attained significant wealth or power. The point is that I pursued it—doggedly—and experienced enough of a tiny taste of it to know that in the long term it wouldn't fully satisfy.

STUCK

For me, this realization—and my confusion about what to do about it—led me to a confession.

After yet another Sunday setting up the bouncy castle, I knew something had to change. When it came to my faith, the title of the old B. B. King song summed it up: "The Thrill Is Gone." The same was true of my work. What used to be interesting and invigorating had become stale. Closing a big deal felt more like relief than cause for rejoicing. Although I had gotten my "get into heaven free" card, my soul was still polluted by the world. I worshipped God on Sundays, but worshipped Wall Street the rest of the week. I did not want to admit it, but faith for me, though genuine, was something of an add-on to an already busy life. This same busyness with work, family, and other responsibilities prevented me from thoughtfully assessing my life and strategically rethinking how I should live.

Somewhere in all of this frustration, I came across a quote widely attributed to writer, professor, and clergyman Henry Van Dyke: "As long as habit and routine dictate the pattern of living, new dimensions of the soul will not emerge." I knew that if I wanted my life to be different—to finally experience joy—I had to change the pattern of my life. But how? Every minute of my life was spoken for, so adding more stuff—even spiritual stuff—seemed out of the question.

I had no room in my life for what my soul desperately needed, and I finally confessed that I was seriously stuck.

Someone once said that when you're at the end of your rope,

God reaches out and offers you a hand. In my case, He used the 10th Mountain Division of the United States Army. This light infantry division trained in the mountains of Colorado to prepare for deployment to the Alps during World War II. They left behind a number of remote cabins that are now operated by the 10th Mountain Division Hut Association and are available to individuals and groups who want to hike, snowshoe, or cross-country ski and enjoy roughing it in the higher altitudes of the Rockies.

When a group of friends asked Michelle and me if we wanted to join them for a getaway in one of these cabins, I was more than ready. Getting away seemed like exactly what I needed to sort out things about my life. And the word *getaway* is used literally here because these rustic cabins are out in the sticks. No running water or electricity. No television or cell phone coverage. Just the crisp mountain air, spectacular views, and each other.

We must have all been on the same wavelength because our conversation quickly turned to matters of faith—specifically how we felt it wasn't delivering what we thought it would. After a lot of lively discussion about everyone's situation, the problem that I was specifically wrestling with emerged as crystal clear as the mountain air: It wasn't Christianity that was the problem. It wasn't my church or even the bouncy castle or the boredom of my work. It was me. I wanted to *have* faith, but I didn't know how to be *transformed* by that faith. I wanted to add some faith to my life, but on my own terms. Romans 12:2 challenged me: "Do not conform to the pattern of this world, but be transformed by the renewing of your mind. Then you will be able to test and approve what God's will is—his good, pleasing and perfect will."

Simply put, the lure of wealth had a firm grip on me, and that was the worldly pattern I was conformed to. I wanted the peace and joy God has promised, but I was afraid to make the hard choices to spend more time with Him because time with Him was time away from work and all my other obligations and hobbies. I wanted all the good stuff that God had to offer, but I was unwilling to let go of other things. I was okay improving my life with a little God sprinkled in, but wasn't so sure I wanted Him to transform it. Ultimately, I knew I had to renew my paradigm and priorities about what I really wanted out of life. So I made a commitment to start renewing my mind by reading the Bible every day for sixty consecutive days.

Of course, since I had become a Christian, I knew that reading the Bible was important, and I tried to read it regularly. But in reality, my Bible reading was sporadic and inconsistent. Something I did mechanically, not something that was fundamental to my joy. Some days I'd read a whole chapter. Most days I'd read a few verses as I waited for the toast to pop up before I headed out the door. And on more days than I'd like to admit I didn't read the Bible at all. It's not that I didn't think it was important. I was just too busy. I only read it when I had time, which was not all that often. I was not only infrequent in my reading, I was ineffective at it. I needed to carve out enough time not just to read but to truly understand what I was reading. Truth be told, I was also waiting for God to wow me with spiritual insight and surprise me with unspeakable joy because I didn't have the guts to challenge the stubborn, selfish, culturally shaped, and flawed thinking that was actually working against the very things I craved—joy, peace, fulfillment.

I made another commitment at 11,600 feet above sea level: I was going to create the margin to dream. To see if I could cobble together a new vision for my life. A life that would get me fired up and out of my funk. I was frustrated and confused enough to finally get serious about taking the time to address this smoldering discontent problem of mine.

And then we had to come down off the mountain.

It's one thing to commit to a course of action when you're dreaming with your friends on a mountaintop. It's another thing to actually do it. We call it good intentions. It's why you can't find an empty elliptical machine at the gym in January but can take your pick in February. Working out takes a commitment. So does reading the Bible in order to understand the true nature of God and the principles of life that lead to lasting joy. So does developing a new vision for your life.

I wasn't sure how I was going to follow through with what I had agreed to, but I wanted it badly enough and was determined to make it happen. I didn't need to be held accountable. I was finally willing to suffer the pain to get to the gain.

THE TROUBLE WITH MARGIN

Margin in our calendars means having or creating extra time in our lives to do something other than the things we are currently doing. The problem is that most people (my "2005 self" included) think creating margin is a matter of time management and delegation strategies. Although some of that may be required in our journey toward joy, the real challenge lies deeper in our hearts. The problem with an efficiency paradigm toward margin is that while it helps us do what we are already doing faster, it is not helping us get rid of the things we shouldn't be doing in the first place.

The best way to significantly build margin into our calendars is to go beyond the time management approach and explore the personal values approach. The clearer we are on our values, our priorities, and our calling, the easier it is to say no to things that don't fit the big picture of where we want our lives to go. I often tell clients, "If you want capacity in your calendar, get conviction about your calling." When you have a compelling vision of the future, and you sense it's God's calling on your life, it's easy to look at your calendar and see the things that aren't supporting the direction you want to go. Saying yes to one thing means saying no to something else. It's best to acknowledge right now and forever that making truly important and big decisions in your life will always involve some level of angst and trade-off. If you're not clear on your values and priorities, you will say yes to anything that even remotely hints at joy. The problem is that few things lead to lasting joy.

I've heard people say things like, "I'd love to take an hour leisurely reading the Bible and praying every morning, but mornings are crazy with the kids, getting them to school, and me getting off to work." (By the way, who said morning was the only time we're allowed to read the Bible?) People also declare that the craziness of their lives is what is preventing them from volunteering, exercising, eating well, spending time with their kids, or doing any number of other good things. And yet, some of the busiest people I know seem to have no problem taking up golf, learning to sail, starting a new business, writing a book, or engaging in new projects that interest them. People will always find a way to create margin for what's important to them and what they value.

Such was the case of one of my coaching clients. When I first met him, he said he had been stuck in a cyclical pattern of life with no joy or purpose for six years. As I asked him about his life, I realized he had a small but fast-growing insurance business with clients and employees all over the country. He didn't have a COO to help with the business, and he didn't even have a personal assistant. I also found out he and his wife were running the financial stewardship program at their church. And to top it all off, they were raising three busy teenagers. No wonder he was stuck. He never had time to intentionally think about his life. Socrates said, "The unexamined life is not a life worth living." My client could vouch for that.

Ultimately, the status quo was so painful that he hired a COO and a personal assistant. This cost him some serious money. Training and supporting them cost him some extra time early on too—things actually got busier before he started to realize the extra margin from delegating to them. But eventually some space started to open up in his calendar and joy started to percolate in his life. He found he was able to actually dream about his life again. New options and rhythms for living his life started to seem possible. His energy—and his joy—were on the upswing. He became more aware of those in need around him, and he enjoyed having the space in his life to help them.

And then he did something really gutsy: he started dedicating one whole day per month to do nothing but get quiet, be prayerful, read the Bible, and think about his life. There is no way he could have done this if he hadn't had enough pain to compel him to create the space in his calendar. He told me that these days became so rich and rewarding that they became the highlight of his month. God started stirring his heart, and creative ways to make a difference in his world beyond work and his family gradually came into focus for him. He knew what he really wanted in his life now, and he knew what he wanted his life to count for in the long term. Over time, he was able to completely restructure his life and get all his values in sync with God's calling. He's having the time of his life!

None of this joy would have been tapped into if he hadn't made the courageous choice to step off the worldly treadmill and rethink the values and priorities that were driving his decisions and direction in life.

Slowing down, serving others, and growing closer to God are the last things Satan wants us to do. Remember, B.U.S.Y. = Burdened Under Satan's Yoke. He wants to keep us busy so that there will be one less Joyful Follower growing the kingdom of God.

REDEEMING "FLIGHT TIME"

It was 2005 when I was finally ready to make some hard trade-offs with how I spent my time. In those days, I traveled almost weekly from Colorado to Dearborn, Michigan, working on several leadership development projects within various divisions of Ford Motor Company. I used to spend every moment on the plane rides working on proposals, fine-tuning project plans, and building new strategies to generate more business with Ford and the other clients I had in Michigan. After a day of sales meetings, project planning, or facilitating workshops, I usually spent my nights entertaining clients over dinner and then returning e-mails later that night in my hotel room. Leveraging every sliver of available time this way was the only way I knew how to be successful. But the success was losing its attraction, and my life was withering on the vine.

I was finally ready to change things up. I resolved to spend my plane rides digging deep into the Bible, reading books by Christian authors, and dreaming about what life could look like with a the-sky's-the-limit lens. I also committed to stopping all client dinners. If I was going to entertain or sell it would happen between 7:00 a.m. and 5:00 p.m. In the evenings, I would get in a quick workout, eat dinner by myself, and settle into my hotel room to do personal self-assessments, talk to the life coach I was working with, read, research career and volunteer opportunities that fit with my passions, speak with ministry leaders and friends and family on the phone, and journal. The growth that happened to me in six months by changing how I used my flight time and evenings was astounding. My faith was growing. My calling was becoming clearer, my convictions stronger. Joy!

I was learning the truth about how God had ordered the world. The truth about how He views me. The truth about what I *really* wanted my life to look like. And I was plugging away at making that life a reality. Exhilarating momentum!

BUT WAIT, THERE'S MORE

As I have said, margin is more than time management, but it's even more than values and priorities. There's something one level deeper than our values that compels us to work so hard and over-commit ourselves. It's the False Self, which is rooted in fear, guilt, comfort, pride, and/or greed and drives us to act in a way that we desperately hope will lead to the approval of others. Read that sentence again. It's huge.

We'll discuss the False Self in great detail in the self-awareness portion of this book, but it's valuable to camp on this concept right now as it relates to your busyness. For most people, displaying constant busyness is something they do to convince themselves and others of their worth, their abilities, and their sense of responsibility.

So what's really at the root of your busyness? Is it fun, energizing activity and work that is a natural outflow of who you are and what you really believe in?

- Or is it driven by fear?
- Or pride?
- Jealousy?
- Selfishness?
- Greed?
- Boredom?
- The desire to impress others?
- Low self-esteem?

Take a moment and really think about the eight things I just listed. What are the emotions that drive your decisions about how you spend your time? If they are any of those toxic emotions, you can be sure that your False Self is compelling you to hide the imperfect you from others and preventing the real—albeit flawed—you from emerging. If you can come to grips with the fact that God loves you just as you are—and free yourself up from caring what others think of you—you'll be able to identify emotionally draining things in your calendar that are only there for the benefit of impressing others. I strongly encourage you to identify the fearful sources of your frantic life and start responsibly stepping away from the things that are holding you back from being the real you God intended you to be.

Identifying and dealing with what's going on in your heart will help you create more margin in your calendar than any time-management technique ever will. And the benefit of this introspection and honesty will go beyond a looser calendar: you'll be on your way toward real liberation, real courage, real freedom—real joy.

This is really important stuff here. Don't blow past it. Get some help digging into these issues and dealing with them. Lasting breakthroughs to a less frenzied life will only come from honest examination of your heart and understanding what's driving your compulsion to be busy all the time.

A few years ago my family and I took an extended vacation in Spain during a time when that country was experiencing 25 percent unemployment. The US media portrayed the situation as dire. I expected to land in Madrid and see blood in the streets. Some friends even expressed concern about our going there. Other friends remarked that if the Spanish would just work a little harder and stop sleeping all afternoon, maybe they wouldn't be in this pickle.

We spent the last week of our trip with the family of a young woman who had lived with us in Colorado for a summer. This gave us great insight into the mind and lifestyle of the Spanish, and it quickly became clear that they value spending quality time with family and friends more than making a few extra bucks. I have to admit, by the end of the trip, I was really enjoying the afternoon naps and late-night dinners. This is a classic case of how what we value is reflected in where we invest our time.

Margin also gives us time to simply rest, relax, recreate, and rejuvenate. I've heard from other life coaches that rest and relaxation can often cause a sense of guilt to bubble up in women. For men, it's anxiety that often starts to rise to the surface. I've noticed this in my own life. There are at least two reasons for this:

1. For many people, slowing down doesn't seem *useful*. It's that performance thing again. But there is more to life than utility and efficiency—and presenting a false identity to the world.
2. Slowing down doesn't seem very loving, responsible, service-oriented, or helpful. It can seem selfish and self-indulgent. But constant stress and pressure without ever replenishing ourselves decreases our ability to love well and serve well.

Creating margin not only impacts our joy by giving us space to rethink our lives, reset our priorities, and rediscover our true selves. It also gives us the flexibility to respond to those who need us right now. To be a better friend. To go visit someone in the hospital at the drop of a hat. To babysit someone's kids with four minutes' notice. To accept a morning invitation for an afternoon fishing excursion with a buddy.

The challenge with margin is not that we need convincing that we need more of it. The challenge is in finding practical ways—beyond time-management strategies—to create it.

———

Here's a simple, values-based process that might help you get off the treadmill of busyness, start creating margin, and start investing time in things that will help you experience greater joy:

> *Write down your top five values in life. I am not going to give you a list to work from because I don't want to skew or bias your thinking. You know what you value in life. Just write down the five things you value most in life and don't overthink it.*

1._____

2._____

3._____

4._____

5._____

> *With these values in mind, write one sentence that describes each of the following seven elements of your life if they were in full alignment with God's plan, your role in His plan, and your values. What would things look like if everything were perfect in*

Your marriage

Your health

Your faith

Your parenting

Your friendships

Your career and finances

Your service

As you look at the sentences you just wrote that describe those elements of your life in their ideal state, which of those seven elements has the biggest gap between your ideal and current reality? Rank all seven of them below starting with the parts of your life where your "real" is most out of whack with your "ideal."

Biggest Gap between Ideal and Real

_____

_____

_____

_____

_____

_____

Smallest Gap between Ideal and Real

With all of this in mind, analyze your calendar for the last three months. What are four things occupying your calendar that are not serving you and/or others well?

_____

_____

_____

_____

Which of these things can you stop doing immediately?

_____

_____

Which can you responsibly back away from and stop doing within the next three to nine months?

_____

_____

Which should you continue doing, but scale back on?

_____

_____

Which things should you delegate?

_____

_____

With some space in your calendar identified, what things should you do more of? (Hint: What things, if you did more of them, will help you bridge some of the gaps in your life that you identified in your gap analysis on page 58?)

_____

_____

What new things should you start doing to bridge those gaps?

_____

_____

Every decision you just made in this exercise is a reflection of your values—and your theology, by the way. I encourage you to take the time to do this full exercise and experience how getting your values aligned with your calendar can build margin and be the first step toward more joy.

Many people who do this exercise are encouraged with massive breakthroughs in their thinking and how they will refocus their time. Others become discouraged and frustrated because they have such conflicting values, desires, and convictions.

The bottom line is that most busyness is rooted in split loyalties between the popular culture and a kingdom worldview. This creates an uncomfortable dissonance between our values/beliefs and how we actually manage our lives. Fortunately, there's a way to snap out of that stalemate and move confidently in the direction of lasting joy.

SIX

A BIDING

LIFE WITH THE SPIRIT

As you build margin and start to rethink your life, reset your priorities, and recapture your time, I encourage you to reengage with God. To abide with Him. I especially encourage you to do this if you have found yourself in the camp of having divided values and convictions.

But what exactly does it mean to abide? When was the last time you heard that word used outside of a Christian context? It's not a common word in our language today. You probably love your spouse, but did you ever say, "Honey, I want to abide with you forever?"

It's not all that complex, really. To *abide* means "to be with" or "to live with." Abiding with God is what you actually do on the Being axis on the Joy Model. It's what you do to grow in your knowledge of and intimacy with God. I can tell you with full confidence and utmost integrity that this is a sure step toward lasting joy.

This word is a simple yet profound description of the relationship God desires with us. "Abide in Me, and I [will abide] in you" (John 15:4 NKJV). He wants this for His pleasure and ours.

My sixty-day immersion into the Bible is an example of abiding with God. Truth be told, it didn't bring me a lot of joy at first. Getting used to a new routine and carving out the time to read was a hassle. Additionally, some of what I saw in the Word when I really dug into it was painful: when you realize your discontent is mostly caused by your disobedience, well, that's a tough pill to swallow. But recognizing your disobedience—and perhaps more important, recognizing the lies that you are living by—are critical steps toward freedom and joy.

The kingdom principles outlined in the Bible aren't rules designed to rain on our parade. They're loving instructions for living a joyful life. A life filled with peace and purpose: "'For I know the plans I have for you,' declares the LORD, 'plans to prosper you and not to harm you, plans to give you hope and a future'" (Jer. 29:11). If we really want the life we hope our faith will give us, we must abide in His presence and have the guts and discipline to do what the Word says.

Abiding with someone or something other than God will eventually move us away from Him and His perfect plan for us. Our culture offers tempting invitations to abide in all sorts of pursuits. For example, Wall Street tells us that money will make us happy. Hollywood tantalizes us with visions of popularity and promiscuity. Madison Avenue plays the siren song of possessions—if we drive the right car, wear the right watch, vacation at the best resort, we'll enjoy a fulfilling life. If we abide with those messages long enough, they ultimately lead to a bankrupt and tired soul. As with chasing the wind, pursuing joy in these things will leave us empty-handed.

Romans 12:2 calls us to renew our minds. This happens when we replace the values and lies of the popular culture—and our past—with the values and truth found in God's Word. Our minds—and lives—will start to transform as we expose ourselves to, marinate in, and take action on those truths.

Here's how it works:

1. Our lives won't change until we change what we focus on and put our energy into.
2. Our focus and energy won't change unless what we value in life changes.
3. Our values won't change unless our thinking changes.
4. Our thinking won't change unless we start putting the right stuff into our brains in the first place.

It's a pretty simple sequence when you think about it. Garbage in. Garbage out.

The apostle Paul spoke to this in Philippians 4:8: "Finally, brothers and sisters, whatever is true, whatever is noble, whatever is right, whatever is pure, whatever is lovely, whatever is admirable—if anything is excellent or praiseworthy—think about such things." Are those the kinds of things we see in the daily news or hear on the radio or read on the Internet? The apostle Paul clarified the power of abiding in these godly things in the next verse:

"Whatever you have learned or received or heard from me, or seen in me—put it into practice. *And the God of peace will be with you*" (v. 9, emphasis added).

Putting things into practice (i.e., Doing) will contribute to joy, but don't get sucked into thinking godly performance is the pinnacle of joy. That'll get you headed toward the Weary Worker syndrome. There is sufficient joy in just Being with God: "In thy presence is fulness of joy" (Ps. 16:11 KJV).

HOW TO ABIDE

While God and His ways are mysterious, abiding with Him doesn't have to be. The ways in which I abide with God aren't new or revolutionary. You're probably familiar with most of these strategies and disciplines, but I want to give you some concrete ideas to undergird an otherwise nebulous concept. These disciplines are the lifeblood of our faith, especially when they are practiced consistently and properly.

Abiding with Christ is not an obligation that earns God's love. It's an opportunity to experience His love and learn more about His helpful precepts for joyful living. Remember, to abide means to live with. Not just when you feel like it. Not when you think you need a hit of spiritual nutrition. But daily living in the presence of God and with the teachings of the Bible.

Let me share what it looks like for me and where it fits within the Joy Model.

THE JOY MODEL

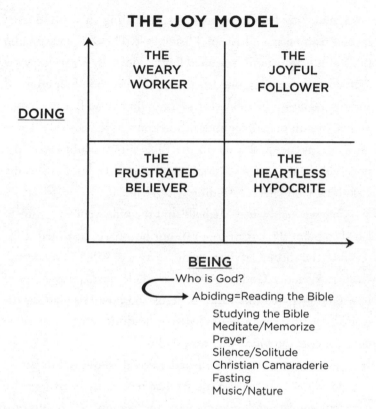

	DOING	
THE WEARY WORKER		THE JOYFUL FOLLOWER
THE FRUSTRATED BELIEVER		THE HEARTLESS HYPOCRITE

BEING

Who is God?

Abiding=Reading the Bible

Studying the Bible
Meditate/Memorize
Prayer
Silence/Solitude
Christian Camaraderie
Fasting
Music/Nature

READ THE BIBLE

One way to read the Bible is to read it like a novel to see the larger picture of God's story as opposed to studying specific passages, word origins, or prophecies from the Old Testament connected to the New. If you're new to reading the Bible, starting with detailed strategies like that can get you lost in the weeds. You might consider purchasing a copy of *The Story*, which strips the Bible of chapters and verses, presenting it much like a novel. When you read the Bible this way, you see more clearly how God has always desired to be with us.

One of my favorite approaches to reading this way doesn't involve reading at all. Instead, I listen to it. There are many audio Bible products. A ministry called Faith Comes By Hearing (www .faithcomesbyhearing.com) has provided more than four hundred audio versions of the Bible that you can download free of charge. When I jump on my mountain bike for a long trail ride, I pop in my earphones and listen to the Bible like I would listen to a novel. Not only does my workout go by quickly, but I'm literally absorbing God's Word. Abiding with Him.

One weekend when Michelle and the kids were out of town, I had to paint the largest room in our house. As I painted, I listened to the entire Old Testament . . . twice. What a wonderful, crazy story about God. It gave me a whole new appreciation of how God prepared the world for Jesus and how His plan for the world is predestined and gradually unfolding. What a boost in confidence about God's love for all of us.

Back in my college days, I had a friend who loved to bet on college football. In one of his weaker moments, he arranged a deceitful hundred-dollar wager with another guy on campus on a game that had already been played, but was not airing on ESPN until later that night. The person who took his bet had no idea the game had already been played. At the half, my friend's team was down by twenty-seven points. The guy he bet against was jumping up and down with excitement while my friend remained calm, knowing his team would eventually rattle off thirty unanswered points in the second half.

Setting aside my friend's temporary lapse in morality, can you see how knowing how the story ends gives us peace even when things unravel in the middle? That's what happens when we understand the larger arc of God's story and we are sure of the ending. No matter what crazy stuff is going on in our lives, we can remain calm and at peace—even joyful.

Here's another example of how understanding and resting in God's sovereign plan brings me peace. Remember my son Neal's episode and how Michelle and I were trusting that "all things work together for good to those who love God, to those who are called according to His purpose" (Rom. 8:28 NKJV)? Well, God came through on this promise: Neal's episode broke him to a point of having to rebuild his identity. His youth pastors and a counselor were so instrumental in healing him that Neal had firsthand experience of the power of God's love flowing through other people. It opened his eyes to the difference others—and he—can make in the life of someone in crisis. In fact, the administration at school often asked Neal if he would speak one-on-one with kids who were going through a tough time.

And so, almost exactly one year to the day of having to rush Neal to the hospital, I sat next to him, fighting back tears of joy, as he registered for college and declared biblical studies as his major so that he can become a pastor. There's nothing more joyful for a parent than seeing a child's worst experience fully redeemed into a great thing just like God's big story promises.

Study the Bible

The Bible, from our cultural perspectives of the twenty-first century, doesn't always make sense. The Old Testament can be particularly confusing. We see the wrath of God juxtaposed to stories of unending love for people. It's hard for people to wrap their brains around that.

In the New Testament, the things Jesus said can seem contrary to so many things we have learned growing up and that we assume to be true. People often refer to this contrarian aspect of Scripture as "the upside-down kingdom of God." "The last will be first, and the first will be last" (Matt. 20:16). "It is more blessed to give than to receive" (Acts 20:35). "Whoever wants to save their life will lose it, but whoever loses their life for me will save it" (Luke 9:24). "The meek . . . will inherit the earth" (Matt. 5:5). It all seems so counterintuitive, which is why we need to dig deep into the text. To thoroughly understand the author, the culture, the people the author is writing to, the real meaning of the words being used, and where a particular section fits into the full narrative of the Bible.

Fortunately, there are thousands of people throughout history who have created tremendous resources to help us study and understand the Bible. My best advice is to go to a Christian bookstore and pick out a good study Bible—one with notes throughout explaining the meaning of the text. If you're really ambitious, get a Bible commentary and a Bible dictionary. Or go online—www.biblegateway.com and www.gotanswers.org are fantastic resources for deciphering what's really going on in the passages you are studying.

Speaking of the Internet, another great way to study the Bible is to listen to sermons. Check out sites like www.sermoncentral.com, www.preaching.com/sermons, and www.biblehub.com/sermons.

But don't just study the Bible. As you dig deeply into the Word, apply it to your daily life. Ask yourself, "What does this mean for me today? How will it change the way I think? How will it change the way I live?" You'll be amazed at how things that are so contrary to popular belief actually bring peace and joy and blessing into your life.

I once coached a Fortune 100 executive who decided to move his young family from the comfortable suburbs of western Chicago to Rwanda to work with a Christian microfinance organization. Because I had been intimately coaching him through the emotional, financial, marital, spiritual, and professional elements of his life, it was no mystery to me how he arrived at this radical decision. But I was curious about how his wife got there. When I first met the two of them, her faith was new and she was wading into it one cautious step at a time. I asked my client how his wife got to the point where she was willing to uproot herself and their three young daughters and move to Rwanda. His response: "There's only one explanation: daily, diligent study of the Bible for a year. She just sees the world differently now than how she saw it a year ago."

Researchers at an organization called the Center for Bible Engagement (www.centerforbibleengagement.org) have been studying Bible reading behaviors of more than 200,000 people from twenty countries since 2003. They have identified something they call the Power of the Four: "A key discovery from the CBE research is that the life of someone who engages scripture four or more times a week looks radically different from the life of someone who does not. In fact, the lives of Christians who do not engage the Bible most days of the week are statistically the same as the lives of non-believers."[1]

The truth of the Bible reorients our brains to what's real and what's not, what's lasting and what's not. And it gives us the confidence to risk living our lives differently than what the popular culture says is normal. The result is experiencing life differently than "normal" people do. The year my client and his family spent in Rwanda provided some of the greatest lessons and blessings of their lives.

MEDITATE ON AND MEMORIZE THE BIBLE

Referring to the Bible as the "Book of Law" that was given to the Israelites, Joshua exhorted his fellow countrymen to "meditate on it day and night" (Josh. 1:8). Why? Because, the author continued, "Then you will be prosperous and successful." You may ask, "And why will that happen?" The answer is threefold:

1. As you learn and memorize the lessons, they will be hardwired into your thinking and it will be easier for you to naturally apply that thinking to your life.
2. Living consistently with biblical principles brings supernatural blessings like peace and joy (Ps. 16:11, Gal. 5:22–23).
3. Living consistently with biblical principles is not just about spiritual stuff. At the most practical level, it's a wise thing to do because it instructs us in ways to improve our relationships, careers, health, finances, and everything else in our lives.

So we have reading, studying, and now meditating—all ways to experience the joy of our faith and make improvements in the practical aspects of our daily lives. I pair memorizing with meditating because when you meditate on a Scripture passage, you will likely memorize it by default. And why is memorizing Scripture important? A friend of mine told me his mom made him and his brothers memorize passages of the Bible when they were young. She would say, "It helps to have it in your brain when you really need it and you don't have your Bible with you." Wise woman.

Some Christians are skeptical of meditation, likening it to Eastern religions. Eastern meditation is largely about emptying one's mind in the hope of calming it, focusing it, and detaching from the world. Christian meditation is about emptying our minds too—specifically of all the bad, negative, false, and depressing stuff—but then filling it back up with the truth about how life really works. It simply means focusing on a passage from the Bible, repeating it, thinking about its meaning, letting it sink into your soul. How you do that is up to you. I have a friend who prints out a passage of Scripture and tapes it to his mirror so that when he gets ready for work in the morning, he can read it over and over. He changes the passage each week so that after a year, he has allowed fifty-two key messages from God to deeply influence him. He has managed to memorize many of them.

Some people benefit from an ancient method known as *lectio divina*. Don't let the Latin scare you—it simply means divine reading, or reading to see what God is saying to you. *Lectio divina* is a process of internalizing Scripture that includes reading the passage, meditating on or thinking about it, praying for greater understanding of its meaning, and contemplating or reflecting on what God might be saying to you.

Again, technology can be an aid to meditating on Scripture. Often when I go for a run or ride my mountain bike, I'll download a whole chapter of Scripture and put my music app on "loop" so that it plays that chapter over and over. It's amazing what you gain from a passage when you listen to it twenty times in a row—and how it sticks with you throughout the rest of the day and beyond.

Another simple meditation strategy is to take a certain passage, read it, then go back and ask yourself the implications of its key words and phrases. For example, we all know the Lord's Prayer and can repeat it verbatim. But instead of absentmindedly reciting it, slow down and take note of its implications. I'll walk you through the first half of the Lord's Prayer (Matt. 6:9–13 KJV) as an example of how this technique works:

- "Our Father": Imagine that. He's not just mine. Nor is He solely yours. He's ours. All of ours. And not a brother. Nor a mother nor a friend. But a Father. A good and loving Father. Think about that.
- "Which art in heaven": He rules the heavenly realms. He exists in heaven while the Prince of Darkness still reigns on the earth. What are the implications of that for you?
- "Hallowed be thy name": What does *hallowed* really mean? What's the true, sacred, and holy meaning behind the word *hallowed*? What are some of God's other hallowed names? Healer, Ruler, King, Redeemer, Father, Yeshua, Immanuel, Counselor, Advocate, Jesus.
- "Thy kingdom come": His kingdom has different rules and He is the ruler of that kingdom. He's looking to us to institute the culture of love from His kingdom to earth. What rules are you playing by now? What are you doing to help His kingdom come?
- "Thy will be done": He has a plan. He has a specific

motive and will. What is the actual big-picture plan God has in mind?

And so on. You can use this ten- to twenty-minute process of meditation with any passage of Scripture to let the full depth of God's truth really settle into your heart and mind. Of course, the true benefit of this is to use what you are learning to challenge your own assumptions about life, the ways in which you see the world, and patterns of thinking and behavior that do not serve you well.

I often use the word *marinate* when I talk about abiding with God's Word, because it really captures what happens when we meditate. I love to barbecue, and when I marinate a steak in a special sauce, the meat takes on the flavor of that sauce. Meditating allows us to take on the flavor of God—to become more like Jesus, to be transformed over time.

For me, reading, studying, meditating on, and memorizing the Bible has not only helped me understand God's sovereign plan and equipped me to quickly recall His truths, it has caused a very real heart shift in me. Like I said earlier, my friends from high school and college are scratching their heads over who I have become. The Bible has changed me at an emotional, psychological, spiritual, and practical level. Real humility and true gratitude have percolated up into my heart over time. I sleep better, breathe easier, and dream bigger now than I did even ten years ago.

I am humbled because I have been so clueless for so long about how to live a purposeful and loving life. I am grateful because God has so generously spelled out a formula for joyful living. The Bible is God's instruction manual for marriage, parenting, friendships, finances, prayer, physical health, emotional health, and business.

For me, learning to engage in these spiritual practices—and then applying the insights to the practical parts of my life—has been similar to my experience with the game of golf. As a former baseball player, I used to hold a golf club like a batter holds a bat. After years of slicing the golf ball, I was at my wit's end. I was humbled. A golfing buddy of mine asked one day, "Are you ever going to learn to play the game correctly?" I confessed that I needed his help. He adjusted my grip in a way that was so foreign and so uncomfortable that I thought I'd either break my wrists or let loose of the club as I swung it. When I told him this, my kind and loving friend said, "Just shut up and trust it." On my very first swing, the ball went straight down the fairway. I went from humble to grateful to joyful in about two minutes.

Today I don't always hit the ball straight down the fairway, but when I do slice or hook it, I know the adjustments I need to make. And my swing feels more natural now. Abiding in God's Word has, over time, helped me develop new "swing thoughts" for my life. It has helped me make adjustments in my daily thinking and living in order to experience the joy that I desire.

PRAYER

Could you imagine living with someone but never talking with that person? Abiding with God is more than spending time in His Word. It's spending time *with* Him, and the way we do that is through prayer. Conversation. Talking to Him and listening to Him. Prayer is a powerful instrument for knowing and experiencing God. It informs our Doing by keeping us focused on His love and how we can pass that love on to others.

My own prayer life has been shaped by two concepts from

Scripture: the Still Prayer: "Be still, and know that I am God . . ." (Ps. 46:10), and the Unceasing Prayer: "Pray without ceasing" (1 Thess. 5:17 NKJV).

Being still, for me, means going to a place where I know I won't be interrupted for twenty to thirty minutes. I'll read or listen to a short passage of Scripture and then set my phone alarm. I sit in a comfortable chair and settle down my heart, mind, and body. I do everything possible to keep from moving my body for that full half hour, not even to shift my weight or scratch an itch on my cheek. It sounds a little extreme at first, but it helps me focus.

Once settled, I start a conversation with God, following the familiar P.R.A.Y. acronym that you may have heard of before:

I **praise** Him by counting all my blessings. Going through all the good things in my life and thanking Him for those blessings: I'm breathing. I can walk. I can see. I know I'll have food to eat today. I have people in my life who care about me. I have meaningful work. I have been given the unmerited gift of salvation. Thank You, God!

Next I **repent** of all the thoughts and actions that distance me from God or hurt others. The word *repent* means not just to confess but to change how we think. In some parts of the Bible, *repent* specifically means to start thinking like God thinks. Once I've exhausted my embarrassing list of things to repent of, I quiet my mind and ask God to search my heart for the things I am doing that are separating me from Him, or hurting me or others, that I am not even aware of. He always seems to reveal some additional habit or negative thought pattern that doesn't serve me, God, or others well. And I repent some more.

And then I **ask** boldly and specifically. The Bible says we "do not have because [we] do not ask God" (James 4:2). Jesus talked about our asking in John 15:7: "If you abide in Me, and My words abide in you, you will ask what you desire, and it shall be done for you" (NKJV). Wait. Stop. Read that it again. It's almost preposterous. Can Jesus really make that claim?

The truth of this statement hit home for me in a beautiful way one night while camping high in the Rocky Mountains. When my youngest son, Quinn, was twelve, he and I went hunting and fishing in the Flattops Wilderness of Colorado. A "Cast and Blast" trip, as I like to call it, in my favorite part of the entire world. I read John 15:7 to him and asked him what he thought. After thinking through it for a while, he said, "You know, Dad, God's pretty smart. He knows that if we really remained in His words we'd start to think just like Him and we'd never ask for anything stupid." The more I thought about it, the more I realized how spot-on he was. "You know, Quinn," I said, "you're right. God is pretty smart . . . and so are you."

We not only need to ask more often and with the right intentions, we need to ask with belief. We can confidently ask God to do something if it is consistent with His will. When we ask from this paradigm—which I have yet to master—God will deliver more than we ever imagined.

Will there be times when a specific prayer seems to go unanswered? For sure. And that's when we need to trust that God must have a larger plan in place that we aren't fully appreciating.

And so when I pray, I ask. I ask hoping that my will is in rhythm and sync with His will.

I ask Him to release me from all condemnation for my sins.

I ask Him to remove any negative thinking or lies that are holding me back in life.

I ask Him not to just forgive me of my sins but to free me from the desire to sin.

I ask that He fulfill all my dreams and wishes and aspirations.

I ask that He help me live with no selfishness or fear.

I ask for patience and compassion.

I ask for many things for many people I know who are struggling in life.

Last, I **yield**. "Not as I will, but as You will" (Matt. 26:39 NKJV). I hand all these issues and requests over to Him. I hold on loosely to the results, trusting that His plan—most likely a little different from mine—is better for everyone involved. I yield knowing that He loves me. I simply detach myself from my fears and desires and hand the outcomes over to Him.

It's typically during this part of my prayer time that I sense Him speaking to me. I shift from speaking to listening. I have never heard an audible word from God, but that doesn't mean He never speaks. It's usually a conviction I sense in my gut or a passage of Scripture that comes to mind that I know I need to pay attention to. That's how I usually hear from God.

It's at this final stage of my Still Prayer discipline that I follow what Henri Nouwen teaches in his wonderful little book *The Way of the Heart*: I relax and "settle my mind down into my heart." Just be quiet. Not straining to hear. Nor wrestling with the urge to speak. Just being. When I'm done, I'm refreshed, focused, and calm.

My Unceasing Prayer strategy was shaped by a classic book called *The Practice of the Presence of God* written by a French monk in the sixteenth century known only as Brother Lawrence. This easy read tells of Brother Lawrence's daily walk with God. Every step he took, every chore he did, and every interaction he had with another person was a combination of prayer, love, and worship. He lived his days with Jesus right next to him.

It's more like a state of being and consciousness than mental dialogue or the recitation of prayers.

I try to do this as I wake up, shower, get dressed, eat breakfast, make school lunches for the kids, work, give a talk, write, go to the store, do chores, work out.

Am I 100 percent consistent? Hardly. But when I am in this loving zone of thinking and being, I experience the joy that God intends for me. I am also more likely to be a blessing to those I interact with.

As you go through your day, imagine Jesus right next to you. In your car on the commute to work. At your desk or wherever it is you work. Imagine Him being with you in a meeting, eating lunch with you. It's a constant companionship with God who is with you always.

I share these tips and techniques as examples that may be helpful for you. Don't get constricted by the details of what I do. Find what works best for you to speak to, listen to, and be with God.

SILENCE AND SOLITUDE

Most of the Christian coaches I know tell me that the discipline of silence and solitude is the most intimidating—yet most useful—abiding strategy for their clients. I agree. It tends to bring the biggest insights and breakthroughs.

When I say silence and solitude, I mean extended time alone with God, your Bible, a journal, and nothing else to distract you. Extended time for most busy people is a longer lunch break. Maybe skipping out of work a little early for some "me" time. But if you really want to connect deeply with God, thoughtfully analyze your heart, and strategically think about your life, you'll likely need more time. I often recommend people regularly take a full twenty-four hours to get away for the sole (soul) purpose of abiding with God. I do it once a quarter, and I also design a summer retreat of three days in the mountains to read, pray, and write. (Okay, maybe I take occasional breaks to chase some trout.)

A retreat like this—what I call a solo silent retreat—will be awkward at first and even seem counterproductive. When I recommend it to my clients, they are universally skeptical. How do you move forward by retreating? Especially all by yourself? But when they try it, to a person they describe it as a pivotal experience in their spiritual growth. If you have a coach or mentor, make sure that person is clear on your goals and challenges so he or she can help you build a strategy that works for you.

I can honestly say that the solo silent retreat is the single most powerful exercise I can recommend when it comes to understanding who you are and how God uniquely wired you for His purpose.

Consider the effect it had on my friend Ron, who is one of the most humble and selfless guys you'll ever meet. He was trying to sort out some major issues related to his life, and I recommended he take off for a couple of days to pray, listen, read, think, and journal. I could tell he wasn't thrilled with my counsel because he is a busy senior executive of a multinational pharmaceutical company with a wife and three kids. But he went anyway, if begrudgingly. When he got back, I asked him how everything went, and he told me he learned something about himself that both surprised and disappointed him.

> God showed me that I am absolutely wracked with selfish ambition. What's more, He showed me how I've become a master at hiding it from others. My ability to subtly get things my way, pat my back, and toot my own horn is the antithesis of the leader I want to be in my life. All my striving and posturing are rooted in fear and low self-esteem, and it's slowly draining the life out of me.

That's some heavy stuff. I was as surprised as he was, because Ron seemed to be a walking example of that little phrase that convicts the rest of us: "God first, others second, yourself last." Which only proves how easy it is to deceive ourselves and others.

During his retreat, as his busy mind slowed down, Ron started to uncover the lies that were shaping his thinking, and once he identified them, he was able to hand them over to God and liberate himself by trusting that selflessness is the path to success in all aspects of life. What followed was immense freedom and joy. He redefined his Being and redirected his Doing. He's now ten times the leader, husband, and dad that he used to be. He's living boldly, generously, and joyously.

Here are a few ideas for structuring your solo silent retreat:

1. First things first: get it on your calendar. Let your spouse, family, employees, boss, coworkers, etc., know that you'll

be spending a day (or two . . . or three) alone and won't be reachable. With all the stakeholders in your life aware of your plans, you can rest easy and commune with God with peace of mind.

2. Go someplace secluded and comfortable—a lake house, beach house, campsite, mountain cabin, etc. Any place that is quiet and where you can be alone will work. Don't do it at home where you will be distracted by visitors, the phone, household projects, and a thousand excuses that get in the way of being alone with God.

3. Shut off your cell phone. No TV either.

4. Give yourself at least an entire day; an overnighter is even better.

5. Bring a journal, a Bible, maybe some music, perhaps one book by a Christian author. That's more than enough. You're not there to Do, but to Be.

6. Take walks. Get outdoors. Get your body moving. Let your surroundings remind you that God created it all for our enjoyment.

7. Journal your thoughts throughout your time alone. Later you can look back and remember what you were thinking and feeling during this time. You'll see patterns, themes, blessings, and, over time, the journey the Lord has taken you on. Let these three "big questions" focus your journaling: "What do I want to say to God, what is God trying to say to me (through prayer, Scripture, or the Christian book I am reading), and what implications does this have for my life?"

8. Relax and enjoy your time. Don't feel like you have to be

praying, reading, and journaling 24/7. Take a nap. Listen to music. Slow down and decompress.

9. Be thoughtful about what you eat and drink. Too much caffeine, sugar, alcohol, nicotine, etc., can distract you and distance you from God.

10. Expect Satan to try to derail you, especially right before you leave. Guard this time ruthlessly. We have an enemy, and the last thing he wants you to do is get your life in alignment with God's will.

CHRISTIAN CAMARADERIE

Abiding with God is not only a solitary endeavor. It is also done in community with other believers. That doesn't mean you abandon good friends who have not yet seen the need for Jesus in their lives. But when it comes to abiding, we need the encouragement and accountability that come with having a few good friends who love God, are spiritually mature, and enjoy getting together to live life.

One of the most rewarding aspects of my life right now is the group of friends Michelle and I have. These aren't Bible study friends. They're just good old-fashioned friends who also happen to be rock-solid Christians. Their insights and practical life counsel and camaraderie keep me centered.

On the flip side, be careful not to isolate yourself into a Holy Huddle lifestyle where all you do is hang out with other Christians. Abiding also means going where Jesus went, and He spent a lot of His time hanging out with sinners because, as He explained, "It is not the healthy who need a doctor, but the sick" (Luke 5:31). Do you have some work or social circles where you can be helpful to people and meet their felt needs? Where you can tell people about Jesus? Where you can be challenged to defend your faith with skeptics, agnostics, and atheists? When I live out my faith in those environments, I sense God's presence just as strongly as I do when I'm with my Christian friends. The key is to find a balance that allows you to abide with God in both settings.

One thing Michelle and I do eight to ten times a year is host a "Cabernet and Conversation" evening at our house. Our Christian friends invite believers and nonbelievers to our house for an evening of conversation. The price of admission is a bottle of wine and an appetizer. After an hour of mingling, we gather everyone together and toss out a simple question that everyone can discuss. The question changes for each gathering: "What's the coolest thing that's happened to you in the last month?" "What's the greatest insight you've had about yourself in the last month?" "What's the biggest lesson you've learned about life in the last six months?"

As our Christian friends respond, they unconsciously display how God is active and living in their lives. Our non-Christian friends share from different points of view. In the end, all of our eyes are opened, God becomes real, and we all connect at the heart level. God is remarkably present in these gatherings and empowers us to demonstrate to our unbelieving friends a winsome picture of our faith.

I have another group of Christian comrades whom I meet with on the first Friday of every month. It's all men. It's not a Bible study. It's not a book study. We all set yearly goals and then get together to review how we're doing and how life is going. We encourage, commiserate with, brainstorm for, challenge, and pray for each other.

One of the most powerful things we try to do is force

ourselves to never share an opinion. Opinions don't count. We try to make sure every idea and comment is backed by Scripture. With a group of spiritually mature men, this works well.

One other helpful rule of thumb we try to uphold: no whining or pontificating about politics, economics, or social issues unless you plan on doing something about it. It keeps us focused on our sphere of influence and what God can do through us.

Fasting

Fasting is one of the long-lost disciplines of the Christian faith that we sadly get little preaching and teaching on these days. The practice of abstaining from food and drink is seen throughout the Old and New Testaments. Fasting is a discipline that can be done simultaneously with all these other abiding disciplines, and, for me, it amplifies their effects.

Jesus Himself fasted for forty days in the wilderness while being tempted by Satan. And throughout the history of the church, people have fasted and prayed to remind themselves to think in God's terms and not in the world's terms. The Catholic and Orthodox churches have fasting days built into their liturgical calendars for this very reason.

Jesus said, "When you fast, do not look somber as the hypocrites do, for they disfigure their faces to show others they are fasting. Truly I tell you, they have received their reward in full" (Matt. 6:16).

There are two things to note here. The first is that Jesus said, "*When* you fast," not "*If* you fast." Fasting is more than a recommendation. It is an expectation. Here's why: our daily comfortable living can numb us, harden our hearts, and make us lose touch with our responsibility in advancing God's kingdom on earth.

We're all guilty of the same pattern: when things are hunky-dory, we forget about God and others and we slide into selfishness and self-reliance. Then, when trouble shows up in one form or another, we're on our knees begging for direction, help, and solace.

The second thing to note about Matthew 6:16 is that there is a reward that comes with fasting. Remember, Jesus never tells us to do things to make us miserable. Everything He asks of us is for our own good and blessing.

Paul warned the Philippians about people who live this way: "Their destiny is destruction, their god is their stomach, and their glory is in their shame. Their mind is set on earthly things" (Phil. 3:19).

Fasting is a way to intentionally disrupt our comfort and make us more mindful of God and more loving to others. The danger zone with fasting is when we get focused on the discipline and forget the *reason* for the discipline. Isaiah pointed this out brilliantly in Isaiah 58:5–9. *The Message* version nails it:

> *Do you think this is the kind of fast day I'm after:*
>   *a day to show off humility?*
> *To put on a pious long face*
>   *and parade around solemnly in black?*
> *Do you call that fasting,*
>   *a fast day that I, GOD, would like?*
> *This is the kind of fast day I'm after:*
>   *to break the chains of injustice,*
>   *get rid of exploitation in the workplace,*
>   *free the oppressed,*
>   *cancel debts.*

He's telling us that fasting is a self-sacrifice that reminds us to love others sacrificially.

My first real attempt at fasting stemmed from a study on Richard J. Foster's *Celebration of Discipline* that I did with a group of men. We had been leaning into all the other disciplines over the course of a year but shared some trepidation about wading into the unknown realm of fasting. Ultimately we decided, "Why not give it a shot?"

I strongly recommend you check with your doctor before fasting if going without food for even one meal produces any unusual physical conditions such as dizziness or lightheadedness. People who are hypoglycemic or diabetic should never fast without consulting their physician.

For my first fast, I planned on having dinner one night and fasting until dinner the next. I was nervous. I committed to only drinking all-natural fruit juices. I chose a day when I didn't have any important meetings because I was afraid my mind might be muddled by low blood sugar and I'd be ineffective. Looking back on it, it's amazing how much I was focused on my comfort and my concern about doing my work well. It was clear I wasn't trusting God to get me through the day.

Two observations came from my first fasting day: (1) I could not get my mind off of food, and (2) I got irritable. Really irritable around 3:30 p.m.

As I continue to fast over the years, I use that first observation—my fixation on food—as the trigger to think about God, to thank Him for the blessings in my life, and to pray for others. Instead of being frustrated that I think about food while fasting, I am grateful for those hunger pangs because they draw me back to

God more frequently throughout the day than on days when my stomach is full. This is exactly the intended effect.

As far as the irritability is concerned, I still wrestle with that. Foster claims that whatever emotion bubbles up in us during fasting is the emotion that controls us. For me, it's irritability (the opposite of the spiritual fruit of patience). For others it can be fear, loneliness, laziness, lust, or pride. The value of this insight is that it gives me something specific to ask God to release me from so that I can serve and love others better.

I am still a work in progress. Being aware of this sin tendency keeps me humble. This is one of the rewards I think Jesus was referring to when He talked about fasting, because a humble heart is always a precursor to a joyful heart.

Another reward of fasting is gratitude (also a precursor to a joyful heart). When I finally break my fast, I couldn't be more thankful that I can finally eat. Sadly, for millions of people around the globe that's not an option.

Fasting from food is only one type of fasting. You could choose to fast from alcohol, sugar, or nicotine. My friend Paul McGinnis decided to fast from media and entertainment in the midst of a season of life where he really needed to hear from God to understand what his true calling in life was. He stopped listening to talk radio and sports radio during his commute. He cut out TV completely. No news via the Internet either. He substituted all his commute time with prayer and listening to worship music, the Bible, and sermons. The Lord spoke. Loudly and often. Over time, God gave Paul clear direction on what he is good at, what really energizes him, and how he can make a positive difference in peoples' lives. Drowning out the noise of the media gave Paul the insight and courage to make some career decisions that have drastically improved his level of joy in life.

Life is one grand adventure of learning and growing. If you haven't tried fasting, I'd encourage you to experiment with it. It might just make you more humble, more thankful, more loving, more joyful.

MUSIC AND NATURE

If God is everywhere, the possibilities of experiencing Him are limitless. I like to think that one of the reasons God gave us our senses was to help us abide with Him better. My ears and eyes are pathways to God—and to a different type of joy than what I experience through the other spiritual disciplines.

When it comes to music—whether it's the rocking sounds of my church's band or the strains of Handel's *Messiah* at Christmas—I'm stirred by God in a powerful and unique way.

A similar thing happens to me when I take my little hunting dog, Remi, up into the sagebrush and aspen groves of the Rockies to hunt blue grouse. God designed him to hunt birds, and watching him do that is watching God's glory flow through one of His creations. It really is a sight to behold. That's the case anytime I witness a person or animal doing exactly what they were designed to do—whether it's an athlete, a performing artist, or a flower. It's just raw beauty.

Nature is not just a sanctuary to be with God; it is a manifestation of God. Observing the beauty of God through all of these experiences is like salve on my tired soul.

For you, it might be watching a ballet dancer leap across the stage. Or standing in front of a painting by Monet. Or walking along the seashore. God is present in the beauty and majesty of all that He has created—what better way to abide with Him?

———

Abiding with God moves us from focus on the self to focus on God. It puts things in perspective and keeps us from the toxic and insular thinking that it's all about us. It's not that we aren't important. In fact, we are extremely important—especially to God. He created us just like He created music and mountains. He wants us to be and do exactly as He designed us. There is no greater joy than letting God's love enter us and then emanate out of us in our individual and completely unique way.

Which raises the question: Do *you* know yourself as well as God knows you?

SEVEN

SELF-AWARENESS

WHO ARE YOU REALLY?

I had a blessed epiphany one night in early October 2008. (Oddly enough, I have a history of spiritual growth every autumn.) I had a paradigm shift about a dimension of the gospel that is rarely preached. And rarely experienced. It has to do with "setting the captives free" and answering the "Who am I?" question.

Jesus came to give us eternal life after our physical death, (John 3:16), but He also came to set us free while we are still living. "For sin shall no longer be your master, because you are not under the law, but under grace" (Rom. 6:14). Grace in this verse does not mean forgiveness—the most common understanding of grace. It means power. As in "Lord, please give me the grace to withstand this trial."

It's this second dimension of the gospel—to be not merely forgiven for sin but given the power to be free from sin—that is experienced only when we get the real answer to "Who am I?"

To live with this kind of freedom in our hearts we need to tap into God's grace (His power) to break away from the bonds and delusions of the False Self and start living out of the True Self. The True Self is what the phrase "who we are *in Christ*" actually means.

Let's get clear on a definition: The False Self is the character, personality, title, position, and identity that we have built up for public display over the years. The energy we put into portraying this False Self to the world is rooted in the emotions of fear, anger, shame, guilt, greed, pride, lust, jealousy, etc.

Now here's the rub: People don't just instantly get free from these emotions with willpower. That's like trying to use willpower to change the color of your eyes. People only detach from these emotions and the False Self when they are confident they have a safety net of God's love to fall into.

First John 4:18 puts it this way: "Perfect love expels all fear, NLT" and fear is at the root of all sin and is the driving force of the False Self. We need that safety net of love because when we stop living the False Self, people will judge and reject us. It's this fear of other peoples' judgment that lets greed, pride, lust, shame, guilt, anger, etc., slip into our thinking and drives all of our posturing and posing so that people will see us as likable, lovable, smart, successful, and funny. Over time, we actually start to think this fake persona we have developed over the years is really who we are. We crave acceptance so much that we stifle our True Self to avoid being judged and voted off the island in our family, work environments, and social circles. If we can shift our minds to care only about the opinion of the most forgiving Judge—and care less about others' opinions of us—we'll find freedom from the toxic emotions that drive anti-joy behaviors.

THE JOY MODEL

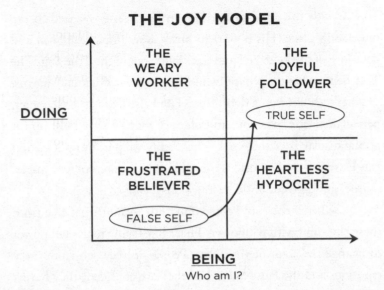

The key to demolishing those toxic emotions (which fall into the category of sin, by the way, because they cause us to miss the mark of God's best for us) is identifying them, admitting they are holding us back, de-powering those sins by confessing them to God and others, and tapping into the power and grace of God. The results are freedom, courage, and joy.

Who cares if people get upset that you've killed your False Self? (Remember, there are many who like and who have come to count on the false you.) Who cares if people don't like your new True Self? You have an audience of One to please. And knowing you're pleasing God is a great feeling.

But if God's boundless love for us remains as our theology, not our reality, we will continue to live in denial and in hiding. We'll go through the spiritual motions, but in our most honest moments we'll still come short of actually feeling freedom and joy in our daily lives. Courage—and grace—in huge doses are required.

Here's a practical way to de-power the limiting beliefs and negative thinking patterns that are rooted in foundational sins such as fear, anger, shame, guilt, greed, pride, lust, jealousy, etc.: The moment you start thinking or acting in a way that is powered by these negative emotions, stop. Take note of the underlying driver of your thinking and acting and remind yourself (i.e., repent/change your thinking) that God knows you have those sins and doesn't hold them against you. He loves you unconditionally. You don't have to hide behind them and prove anything to Him. He's freed you from judgment and condemnation so that you can be free from those negative thoughts. This is the heart of the gospel that we need to remind ourselves of daily.

The apostle Paul described this mind-management strategy like this in 2 Corinthians 10:5: "We demolish arguments and every pretension that sets itself up against the knowledge of God, and we take captive every thought to make it obedient to Christ."

Those negative thoughts are arguments and pretensions that separate us from God. We need to take them captive the second they pop into our heads and crush them by reminding ourselves that Christ forgives us of—and frees us from—those thoughts every day. It takes mindfulness and self-awareness to catch ourselves thinking wrongly so that we can tap into God's grace and get our thinking back on the right track.

ON THE LOOKOUT FOR BAD THINKING

I once coached a talented young businessman who sold his company for millions of dollars. It provided him and his family a wonderful opportunity to rethink their lives and reimagine how he could dedicate his time, talent, and treasure toward building God's kingdom. The process of exploring how he could leverage his gifts in a way that was joyful to him and glorifying to God was slower than he had hoped for. He started to get antsy. He felt the clock ticking. He started looking at options that didn't really fit who he was. As we explored the compulsion that was driving this thinking and direction, he came across the root cause: he was concerned that people would think he was a "one-hit wonder" with his first business, and he believed that if he didn't get busy soon, people would label him as either lazy or lucky or both. This was his fear. This was his self-awareness breakthrough. Moving forward, he had to stay constantly vigilant to moments when this fear would creep into his thinking. Then he'd capture that fear and make it obedient to the truth that Christ knows he's doing his best to serve Him and love others.

Another successful businessman I coached used to wrestle with impatience that would sometimes flame into anger. His self-awareness breakthrough happened when he realized this anger was rooted in low self-esteem. Here's how: He felt that he was neither lovable nor especially talented. So he compensated for this with hard work that would lead to visible and worldly success. And it worked. People revered him. And Christians especially revered him when his financial generosity became so evident. The problem was that when anything or anyone got in the slightest way of his success, he responded with impatience and anger because it threatened his ability to keep up the smoke screen that had so effectively masked his sense of unworthiness from others for so long.

Like the first guy, he needed to constantly remind himself

that he didn't need to prove his worthiness to anyone. God had already deemed him worthy. What a massive relief this breakthrough was for him.

CHILD OF THE KING

One of the best tools I know of for setting people free from limited thinking was devised by a wise Christian counselor named Dr. Ed Laymance. Ed has helped many people grow into full appreciation for who they really are in Christ—who their True Self is. He devised a manifesto that he encourages people to read daily for thirty days. The words correlate to scriptural truth that he recommends people research, study, and meditate on.

This has helped me personally and many of my coaching clients. It's proof that God's Word is more than just instruction. It's truly medicine.

Here is his "Child of the King" manifesto. Read it and be blessed.

**Because of who Jesus Christ is, and because
He is my Savior and my Lord:**

*I am a child of the King of Kings and Lord of Lords,
    (Rev. 1:8, John 1:12)
seated with Christ in the heavenly realm. I am chosen,
    accepted,   (Eph. 2:6, 1 Peter 2:9)
and included—a citizen of heaven and a member of God's
    household.   (John 14:1–6, Eph. 2:19)*

I am loved by God unconditionally and without reserva-
 tion.   *(Rom. 5:6–8, 1 John 4:10)*
I belong to Him, having been bought by Him with the
 (1 Peter 2:9, 1 Cor. 6:19)
precious blood of Jesus. I have eternal life and will be
 (1 John 5:11–13, John 3:16)
saved from all of God's wrath to come—guaranteed!
 (Rom. 5:9, Eph. 1:13–14)
I am a Christian. I am not just different in what I do.
 (1 Peter 4:16)
My identity has changed. Who I am has changed. Everything
 has become brand new.   *(2 Cor. 5:17, Gal. 2:20)*
I am a dwelling place in which God lives by His Spirit.
 (Eph. 2:22, 1 Cor. 6:19)
I have access to Him anytime, anywhere, for any reason.
 (Eph. 2:18, Phil. 4:6–7)
I am God's creation—His workmanship. I was created by Him
 (Ps. 139, Eph. 2:10)
and for Him, so who I am and what I do matters.
 (Col. 1:16, Gal. 6:7–9)
I am spiritually alive. I have been set free from the fear of
 death   *(Rom. 6:8–11, Heb. 2:14–15)*
and have been given life to live and enjoy to the full.
 (John 10:10)
I am forgiven—completely, totally, and absolutely.
 (1 John 1:9, Ps. 103:8–13)
I have been rescued from the dominion of darkness and
 brought into the Kingdom of light—the Kingdom of
 the Son.   *(Col. 1:13)*

I have been set free from the penalty of sin and the power
  of sin.   (Rom. 6:16–23, Gal. 5:1)
I am an enemy of Satan and at war with spiritual forces of
  evil, but   (1 Peter 5:8, Eph. 6:12)
greater is He that is in me than he that is in the world.
  (1 John 4:4)
If God is for me, it doesn't matter who or what stands
  against me,   (Rom. 8:31, Eph. 1:18–23)
because nothing and no one can separate me from the love
  of Christ—not hurt, pain, loss, problem, or broken-
  ness; not persecution, trouble, difficulty, or danger;
  not abandonment, abuse, addictions, or appetites;
  not desires, food, sexuality, or relationships; not life or
  death, angels or demons; not my past, the present, or
  the future; no power, no person, no place, not anything
  in all creation;   (Rom. 8:35–39)
not even Satan himself shall prevail.   (Col. 2:15)
I am in the hands of Jesus, in the hands of God, and noth-
  ing and no one can snatch me out of God's hands.
  (John 10:27–28)
I will fear no evil because God is with me, and
  (Ps. 23:4, 2 Tim. 1:7)
He has promised to never leave me nor forsake me.
  (Heb. 13:5)
God's presence is with me everywhere I go—(Ps. 139:7)
to the heights of heaven, through the valley of the shadow, to the
  ends of the earth—forever and always.   (Matt. 28:19–20)

I am a child of the King and choose this day to live as one.[1]

SELF-AWARENESS OF OUR SKILLS
AND PREFERRED WORK STYLE

A few years ago a gentleman I'll call Tim asked me to coach him through some issues related to integrating his faith into his everyday life. He was retired, independently wealthy, had a strong marriage, maintained good relationships with his kids, and was feeling that tug to do something more with his life—something that would satisfy his desire to "do" Christianity, not just believe it.

He knew the Bible inside and out—the kind of guy who could quote chapter and verse. But in the process of accumulating all that biblical knowledge, he confessed that his life lacked zest and vision. He went to church and did all the right things that church people do. But it was clear that he had a joyless, "go through the motions" faith. He thought that if he started doing "ministry things," his faith would finally deliver what he had hoped for all along.

He shared that he had already misfired on that account—about a year before we met he had accepted the position of CEO for a Christian nonprofit. It was a horrible fit. Talk about being stuck in the upper-left-hand quadrant of the Joy Model. It was bad for him and the ministry. Ultimately, he got fired. He was devastated and embarrassed.

One of the first things we did together was to complete the StrengthsFinder assessment (administered by the Gallup organization). As we went through the results, Tim had one of those "aha" moments and exclaimed, "No wonder I failed so quickly and miserably. I had the right skills, but the way I think and the way I am wired would never work in a culture like that." His low level of self-awareness going into that job led to a valuable, albeit painful, lesson.

Tim was the type of guy who thrived well with a few close and collaborative relationships, but his role in that organization had forced him to manage several direct reports, run interference between board members and donors, and travel to visit the many ministry constituents. Tim was wildly successful in his previous business, and he and the board both thought it would be easy to replicate that success. The fact of the matter, however, was that his successful company never employed more than ten people. It was small, and the relationships were deep. Additionally, he called all the shots in his previous business. Even though Tim was the CEO at the nonprofit, he had a confusing web of stakeholders to keep happy and was handcuffed when it came to making quick decisions.

Increased self-awareness about how God wired him to think and the environments he thrives in released Tim from the shame of that failure and the anger he felt toward the ministry. He wasn't a bad guy or losing his touch or working with idiots. It was clear it was just a bad fit. Those were huge steps toward more joy.

This breakthrough freed him up so much that he developed the courage to do some soul-searching for other blind spots. As he dug deeper, he identified an interesting fact about himself: Although he craved deep relationships, he had gotten really good at artfully shifting relationships away from full vulnerability when things got too chummy. He had limits to his authenticity because he was afraid people would judge him. And so he became very skilled at stopping just shy of really being himself in his friendships. Once he realized this, he knew that if he wanted friends who weren't phony, he had to stop being a phony friend.

Fast-forward to today and Tim now has two real friends. That may sound trivial, but I'm talking about *real* friends. Not acquaintances. And certainly not Facebook friends. Not many people can say that. He is also leading a nonprofit that is tailor-made to his skills and values. If that doesn't describe a giant leap toward greater joy, I don't know what does.

TAKING TIME TO TAKE STOCK

As we saw with Tim, understanding who you are—how God uniquely put you together—is critical to building a life of joy. It involves looking back on your life to see how you got where you are today as well as where you currently sense God is calling you to go. Self-awareness reveals your passions, strengths, blind spots, and environments you thrive in, as well as your fears, selfishness, pride, and worries.

Self-awareness is more than just knowing your skills and talents. It's about knowing how you relate to God, how you communicate with others, how you think and process information, what things you avoid, what you are passionate about, and other components that are unique to you.

It is about rediscovering, reorienting, and releasing your truest, best self to the life and mission God has called you to fulfill.

As it relates to your work and service, when you can focus your best skills on the things you are most passionate about, you will most definitely experience a new level of joy that has previously only been sporadic or has completely eluded you. You'll be zeroing in on your calling—the good works planned in advance for you (Eph. 2:10).

But our lives are made up of more than our work and service. Having greater self-awareness about our communication style, our idiosyncrasies, and our attitudes about money, marriage, parenting, and health can empower us to make thoughtful changes that will improve the full spectrum of our lives.

Lack of self-awareness not only contributes to the frustration we sometimes feel on a particular day, but it can also lead to a lifetime of regret. After spending a number of years tending to the needs of people who were dying, Bronnie Ware wrote *The Top Five Regrets of the Dying*. The most common regret of the people she worked with? "I wish I'd had the courage to live a life true to myself, not the life others expected of me."[2] Of course, we can't be true to ourselves if we have false notions of ourselves.

Higher levels of self-awareness open the door to a life of joy and purpose and impact. It is believed that St. Catherine of Sienna wrote, "Be who you were created to be and you will set the world on fire."

Talk to any life coach and they'll tell you that the pattern that leads to a midlife crisis is incredibly consistent: People start out with lofty dreams and aspirations in their high school and college years, but work, mortgages, ambition, responsibilities, toys, fears, and obligations slowly creep in and overwhelm them. Twenty-five years later, they pop their heads up from their desks and wonder what in the world has happened to them. Somewhere along the way they let the everyday stresses and influences of life change them to the point where they couldn't recall who they were and what they cared about at the beginning of the journey. It happens to all of us. We've layered other peoples' agendas onto our lives and created the False Self. But most don't know it's their False Self because it has slowly become the only identity they know.

We need to get back to God's plan for our lives by reacquainting ourselves with who God designed us to be. For people trying to make this change, it seems like they are leaving their real self, but they are actually *returning* to their real self. Brutal honesty, large portions of courage, and the conviction of God's love are the necessary ingredients for getting out of this trap.

BURIED DREAMS

You may or may not recall how you got off track with your heart, but I remember how I did. It was a cloudless Tuesday afternoon. October 1987. I was sitting at my desk in my first post-college job looking out of the window next to my cubicle in a nondescript, six-story office building in a nondescript office park in a nondescript Chicago suburb.

I was daydreaming and reminiscing. As the son of a high school football coach—and a high school and college player myself—I had spent a lot of time around the game. I can remember vividly getting out of school as a fifth grader, jumping on my bike, and riding through the red, yellow, and orange maple leaves that had fallen on the sidewalks of my little New England town. I can smell those leaves now. I was on my way to the high school to stand next to my dad as he coached. As I got older and started playing, being on a football field became the most natural and relaxed place in the world for me.

As I looked out of the window in my office building, it dawned on me that this was the first Tuesday in October since I was eight years old that I wasn't walking onto a football field at three in the afternoon. My heart had reached a fork in the road. Do I press on and chase the big bucks like all my contemporaries from Amherst College, or do I quit and go coach football somewhere?

Quitting was such a distasteful—even shameful—word to me. Everyone else I knew was "working," moving forward with their lives. To cap it all off, there was a guy where I worked in his early thirties. Young, successful, smart, good-looking, and respected. He had just bought a brand-new Acura—the luxury brand that Honda had launched the previous year. At that very moment I caved to the "deceitfulness of riches" (Matt. 13:22 NKJV) and turned my back on my heart. Which, looking back, astounds me because I never was, and still am not, a "car guy." They just don't matter that much to me. But I thought they should.

It wasn't until years later that I realized not quitting my job was the equivalent of quitting a dream. Many years later, I have come to see God's hand in all this and am able to reconcile things in my mind. Instead of lamenting my decision, I am now aware that God let me go down that path so that I would have twenty years of smoldering discontent that would give me great empathy for those who are struggling to find purpose and joy. God also gave me twenty years of executive coaching and consulting experience in the business world to prepare me for what I am doing now. I ended up being a coach after all—albeit for the game of life instead of football.

HOW DO YOU EXAMINE YOUR LIFE?

Several years ago a well-known health and fitness expert was speaking about obesity to an audience of rather large adults.

He explained that people do not become obese overnight but instead are victims of what he called "creeping obesity." Because the addition of a couple of pounds annually doesn't seem like much, after twenty years no one really thinks they are twenty to thirty pounds over their ideal weight. Rather, they say things like, "I need to lose a few pounds," or "I'm not really obese—just a little overweight." He challenged the group to go home, lock themselves in their bedrooms, take off all their clothes, and stand in front of a full-length mirror buck naked. "Turn to the left, turn to the right—take a good long look, and then decide if you're obese or not." Those who accepted his challenge came back and said things like, "That's the first time I ever really looked at myself that way," or "I kept thinking, *What happened?*" Those who did it were the ones who were most successful in weight loss.

True self-awareness comes with that same degree of brutal honesty. (I'll pause to note here the importance of seeing clearly and accurately. Sometimes we look at ourselves and see flaws that are not really there, or we make the flaws that are there much bigger than they are in reality. That can be just as damaging as ignoring problems altogether.) Peel back the layers of false identity until you see your real self laid bare—the good, the bad, and the ugly. In a way, it's your willingness to strip down in front of the mirror to your soul and pay attention to what you see. Behaviors and thinking that miss the mark of serving you, God, and others well will be revealed. Eventually God's grace and the wisdom of His Word will help you return to the glorious you God originally designed you to be.

OVEREXPOSED

Here's a way to start uncovering issues that you may be hiding or ignoring. Ask yourself this question: What do you know that you are pretending not to know? Be honest. Let's continue the health theme from above as an example. How are you doing in that category? You and I both know that eating less animal fat, consuming more fruits and vegetables, and exercising three to five times a week are important to our health. Some of us also know that our bodies are not our own. Our bodies are temples of the Holy Spirit that were "bought at a price" (1 Cor. 6:19–20). We are supposed to steward our bodies so that we are fit enough to serve and love others. How are you doing in this area of your life? Are you fooling yourself? Do you really think ignoring these issues today won't have a real impact on your joy tomorrow?

Let's try another example: How much of your emotional and mental energy goes toward managing peoples' opinions of you? If you don't deal with your posing and pleasing, you'll eventually suffer the consequences of stress, identity confusion, and placing energy in things that don't serve you well. For the record, I still struggle with this part of my False Self.

I already mentioned the StrengthsFinder assessment, which I think is the best and easiest to use, but there are other assessments, including the Myers-Briggs Type Indicator (MBTI), the Birkman Assessment, Kolbe, and Styles of Influence. All of these, and others, are designed to help you "know thyself."

Self-assessment helps reveal your truest self by reminding you what you enjoy doing, what your predisposition is, what you're good at, how your interests and personality match up to various careers, relationships, and aspirations. While most self-assessment tests are self-guided, I highly recommend debriefing your results with the help of a coach or trusted advisor. A qualified life coach will be able to direct you to any number of self-assessment tools that are best suited to your particular journey. These tests will help you understand who you really are; a coach will help you understand what to do about it.

VOICES OF REASON

Another option—or addition—to getting a coach to help you increase your self-awareness is to form your own personal board of directors to help you confirm your strengths and passions, identify your blind spots, and encourage you. If that sounds too formal for you, simply think of this board as a small group of people who know you well and care about you enough to tell you the truth. For most of us, our spouse is the chairman of the board. As one of my friends recently said to me, "It seems like an odd coincidence, but whenever I hear God's voice, my wife's lips happen to be moving." I know exactly what he means, and you probably do too. Our spouses see us at our best and at our worst, and as much as we may not like to hear it, when they tell us the truth, it's usually for our own good.

For example, every spiritual gifts assessment I have ever taken shows that one of my gifts is wisdom. Whenever I get right down to the root of a challenge or a problem that someone is wrestling with, I have an uncanny knack for seeing clear strategies and steps that make practical and scriptural sense. God's just wired me that way. But according to my wife, there are times when I can come off like a know-it-all. Ouch! Now, she didn't tell me that to hurt my feelings but to protect me, and that sort of feedback is vital to self-awareness. Because I trust her and know she has my best interests at heart, I know that when it comes to wisdom, I may need to reel it in a bit, to not be so quick to jump in with all the answers. Every gift and skill has a dark side. Arrogance is the dark side of wisdom when it is used hastily or without humility. This was my blind spot, and I would have remained blind to it without an honest word from the chairman of my board.

You may be saying, "That's an interesting breakthrough in your self-awareness, Jeff, but what does that have to do with joy?" A lot, actually. It relieves me of the pressure of having to be the "answer man." It forces me to ask the questions that give me the real insight to be helpful instead of making assumptions or trying to fix the problem for the person I'm coaching. It causes the person I am speaking with to call on their own creativity for solutions, which builds confidence in their own abilities, and that brings me joy. My conversations are more relaxed, more effective, more loving, more enjoyable.

If you're not married, seek out a couple of trusted friends—people who do not stand to lose anything by telling you the truth. Tell them you are trying to figure out some things about your life and that you need some honest input, especially about the bad stuff. Or, as I explain to my clients, ask for the feedback they're afraid you'll react negatively to. Then graciously receive it. Don't make excuses or challenge their insights. Accept their words, thank them, and then act on what you have learned about yourself.

A word to those of you who are leaders: Getting honest input is difficult because your positional power creates the fear of retribution if someone tells you like it really is. Promise you'll receive the feedback graciously, and stick to your word. Be prepared to be humbled. I encourage you to welcome it. Humility, like gratitude, is one of the precursors to real joy because humility makes us tolerant of other peoples' faults instead of constantly being irritated with them. Humility also confirms we don't have it all figured out and probably never will. It releases us from the stress of living with the frustrating illusion that we can control everything.

As you invite feedback from others, exercise discernment and choose carefully what you act on. Once, after sharing with a close Christian friend the disconnect I was feeling between my faith and my actual life and where I felt God might be leading me, he let me have it: "Jeff, I know you want to discover your life purpose and all, but you've got three kids, a wonderful wife, you're active in the community, and you're just about to enter your peak earning years. You have a lot going for you, and this direction of yours seems a little irresponsible. Quit trying to live in la-la land where you think life will be perfect on the other side of the fence."

That hit me pretty hard until I realized that the most responsible thing I could do for my family was not to make them comfy and cozy with more stuff and security from my peak earning years. The best thing I could do was to have them see me authentically wrestling with how to follow Jesus, to be true to how He wired me, and to start living a life of adventure and service. The Bible teaches us to seek the counsel of many (Prov. 15:22). It doesn't say we have to "follow the counsel of all."

We've so bought into the materialism of our culture that even our Christian friends might caution us to slow down, be thankful for what we have, and set aside our dreams and passions. Is that the mom or dad you want your kids to see? Is that your truest self?

INTROSPECTION *AND* ACTION

When it comes to increased self-awareness, be careful not to get stuck in introspection mode. If you are truly honest as you examine yourself, you will start to get some clarity on what to do at both the spiritual (Being) and practical (Doing) levels, but rarely will you get full clarity.

The temptation for many is to stay in the introspection mode of building self-awareness for too long. Perpetual navel-gazing. In a way, it becomes a new self-indulgent hobby. One that traps you into inaction.

So get going. Do something. If God is stirring your heart about the homeless, volunteer to serve meals at a shelter. If you have a passion for school children in inner-city schools, go mentor some kids. If it's become clear that the precious time you have with your young kids is slipping away, make sure you figure out a way to invest in their lives. If your finances and giving don't feel right, educate yourself on money management and stewardship.

Moving from introspection to action as a strategy for greater self-awareness is not only helpful for revealing your heart, your thinking, your biases, and your fears; it's invaluable for discovering what you are passionate about.

Bob Buford (author of *Halftime*) calls these small exploratory steps "low cost probes" that will expose you to new ideas and people doing meaningful work in the world.

Without overcommitting and burning up all the margin you worked so hard to create, use smaller chunks of time to—as the saying goes—"let your heart break for what breaks God's heart." Breaking out of your small world will expose you to things that haven't been on your radar. Things that may stir a passion you never thought could be so intense.

One time I was coaching a group of people and one of the guys kept bemoaning the fact that in spite of all the self-awareness tests and assessments he took and all the self-help books he had read, he still couldn't find his true calling in life. Finally, someone in our group spoke up: "Dude, enough is enough. I've listened to you go on and on about not knowing what God wants you to do with your life. Just go do something. *Anything!*"

It stopped him in his tracks. It turns out his mother went to the local homeless shelter every Tuesday morning to make lunches. She was eighty years old. He decided to join her the following Tuesday.

He reported back to the group, "I spent three hours squirting mustard on baloney sandwiches as I talked with the men and women who came into the shelter. I learned so much about their lives, the causes of homelessness, and began to understand their needs. Instead of learning more about myself, I learned about others, and that simple act brought me more joy and energy than I've had in a long time." As a self-made millionaire who used to have disdain for the "lazy homeless," he now knew people didn't wish this plight on themselves. His self-awareness—and his humility, gratitude, and compassion—jumped a notch or two.

Something similar happened to me. I knew that God had good works planned in advance for me to do (Eph. 2:10), but I didn't know what those "good works" were. That's why I first engaged a coach. I remember reading a quote by the philosopher Søren Kierkegaard that said, "The crucial thing is to find a truth which is truth for me, to find the idea for which I am willing to live and die." That quote stung me. Obviously I would give my life for Michelle and our kids, but clearly I didn't have a cause or mission of the same magnitude. My heart yearned for that, but I had allowed it to become calloused over the years. I was stuck in a rut of thinking the whole world revolved around management consulting for the Fortune 500. I needed to get outside of myself—beyond introspection—and into action to discover what makes me mad, sad, or glad. My coach helped me broaden the aperture through which I was viewing the world and helped me find a purpose outside of myself and my family that energized me. If I hadn't started looking outside of myself to see what was going on in the world, I might still be trying to find my life purpose and the joy that comes with it.

As your self-awareness increases, the adjustments you need to make in your life become more obvious. These adjustments will need to take place in your attitude, how you interact with people, and how you spend your time. These adjustments will eventually get you back to the person God originally created you to be.

NOTE TO SELF

As I was in the throes of trying to figure out God's purpose for my life in 2005, I explored everything under the sun. At one point I confessed to my coach that he probably thought I was schizophrenic because I kept bouncing from one crazy idea to the next. He calmed me down by saying he'd be a little concerned if I *wasn't* exploring a wide range of options. He encouraged me to use this time of my life to look under every stone for any clue about how God created me and how I could discover and engage in His calling on my life. He also encouraged me to journal.

I was not then (nor am I today) a natural "journaler," but I can attest to the power of journaling as a method for increasing your self-awareness. I started writing down everything going through my mind. All the things I was learning as I built margin, started abiding with God, and explored who I really was. I wrote three or four times a week. Most of the time it seemed like random stream-of-consciousness writing that wasn't leading me anywhere or surfacing any real patterns or clues. I often doubted the value of taking the time to do it.

But then one day I grabbed my journals and sat in a chair by the stream on our property here in Colorado. I read six months of journaling in two hours. I read all the fears, concerns, hopes, negative thinking, positive thinking, and dreams that had been rattling around in my head. The answer I had been searching for jumped off the page for me: God had prepared me to free people up to know His love and purpose for their lives so they can make a positive difference in the world and live with greater courage and joy.

Grasping this deep-down conviction about what to do with my life continues to be one of the most joyful, reassuring, and energizing aspects of my life. I pray you get to experience that one day.

SPEAKING OF COURAGE

Bob Buford often asks people who are serious about discovering God's calling, "Who gave you permission to start dreaming again?" It's a playful question that exposes a sad truth: most adults stop dreaming by their mid-twenties.

Instead of analyzing the social and psychological reasons for this, let me simply ask you one of the oldest, most clichéd coaching questions known to mankind. If your coach hasn't asked you this question, shame on them. If you haven't thought seriously about this question, shame on you. Here it is: If time, money, and failure weren't obstacles, what would you do with your life?

I know this question is old and tired, but I strongly encourage you to dream—no holds barred—about how you would live your ideal life. I challenge you to take fifteen minutes to write down what the ideal day, week, month, and year of your perfect life would look like. Don't write thinking that you have to impress or appease anyone. Just write from the heart. You won't have to share this with your pastor, small group, or even your spouse. Be honest with yourself.

You may be concerned that it seems far-fetched, hedonistic, or unrealistic. I don't care. Just keep writing. When you're done, take a step back from what you wrote and layer one extra question onto what you wrote: "How can I live this dream *and* make a positive difference in peoples' lives and glorify God?" You may already have these two elements woven into your ideal life description. If not, this one extra question—applied *after* all your dream writing—will ensure your dream isn't leading you toward the self-indulgent dead end of secular happiness. Real joy is being exactly who we are *in service to others and for the glory of God*. This exercise remains one of the most powerful self-awareness exercises for people seeking lasting joy in their lives.

Once you understand what makes you tick, what you are passionate about, what fears are holding you back, and how you can serve God and others doing it, you are well on your way to experiencing true joy and fulfillment. The life you've always wanted is just around the corner.

Unfortunately, a powerful force lurks in the shadows. One that can completely derail you from your new adventure.

EIGHT

TREASURE

THE GREEN MONSTER

I once asked a life coach what he believes is the number one reason people hold back from courageously pursuing the lives that
will lead them to true joy. He didn't hesitate for a second: "It's the
Green Monster." Now, as a kid from Massachusetts, I thought he
was referring to the left field wall in Fenway Park. It took me a
second to realize he was talking about money, not the Red Sox.

So let's shoot straight here: Doing what you know in your heart
you need to do to build a life of greater joy could cost you. Either in
the form of less income earned, investments sold, savings tapped, or
shiny new things not purchased. The good news is that if you really
get yourself to the place where you can authentically be who God
has created you to be, money issues won't dominate your thinking.

Don't get me wrong. I enjoy the things that money can buy.

This is not a call for you to start shopping at Goodwill or to trade in your Benz for a bike. Money can contribute to joy, but not nearly as much as we think.

In fact, a recent study of US adults showed that while money matters, the incremental impact on a person's joy starts to diminish dollar for dollar after the $75,000 annual income mark.[1]

In another ongoing study, Martin Seligman, the author of *Flourish*, notes that "life satisfaction in the United States has been flat for fifty years while GDP has tripled."[2]

Growing in your belief—at a spiritual, emotional, and intellectual level—that money and joy are not as correlated as everyone thinks is a huge step toward joy, freedom, and courage.

Releasing your death grip on money frees you to start creatively realigning your life with your passions and God's larger plan. And who knows, the adjustments you make may lead to *more* money than you currently have. I've seen plenty of people make significant, exhilarating, and self-sacrificing changes in their lives and have their incomes go up. There are no shortage of ways to attach revenue streams to lives of purpose and passion.

Over time, it has become clear to me why money so often robs us of our joy. Why some of the wealthiest people are also some of the most miserable. Warped paradigms about money—and how money communicates to the world who we are—are two root causes of much angst.

For some people, the stress of making the monthly nut is the primary joy robber. I coached a guy once who made $300,000 a month whose lifestyle and debt situation had become incredibly complex. His level of stress was identical to the single mom barely scraping by on $25,000 a year.

For other people, the challenge is the fear of not having enough in old age. An estate-planning friend of mine said that one of his clients was living in fear, convinced by his financial advisor that if he didn't have $20 million in investable assets by retirement age then he would surely be destitute at the end of his life. I learned a long time ago that if something doesn't make sense, follow the money. That advisor stood to profit greatly from his client's investments.

The most common reason I hear from coaches about why finances degrade their clients' joy has to do with identity and pride. Most people—especially men—measure their self-worth based on their incomes. This is wrongheaded, of course, but completely understandable, since most of those same men judge other men based on *their* incomes! The question here becomes: Are you strong enough not to care about what others think about you? I submit that you will be strong enough not to care the moment you realize the stress of keeping up—or the emptiness of staying ahead—just isn't worth it.

HOLLOW VICTORY

The notion that trouncing the Joneses will not make us happy is hard for people to grasp when they are young. When I first read in the Bible that King Solomon said all of his amassing of wealth was nothing but vanity and a chasing of the wind (Eccl. 2:26), I remember saying to myself, "I'm okay chasing the money and risking that maybe he's right. I could live with that problem." I was okay with that until my values and dreams and aspirations started to shift around age forty. The cost of playing by the rules of popular culture and keeping up appearances started to become too high for me. It was holding me back from what I really wanted to do with my life. The disconnect between how I wanted to live my life and the life I was actually living was great enough for me to risk making some changes that could threaten my net worth. As I have written earlier, we get serious about change when the pain of our status quo becomes intolerable.

If you are content with your life and your finances, this may not make sense to you yet. It may never make sense to you. But for me, there were too many people before me who had come to King Solomon's same conclusion.

Here's one way to think about it: Recall a time when someone told you something that just didn't make any sense at all. And years later, as you got older, it dawned on you that they were right after all. This is how I look at money. I'm trusting that meaningful work, a strong marriage, a deeper faith in God, good relationships with my kids, and a small group of friends will mean more to me on my deathbed than my W-2s.

MONEY *AND* JOY: YAY!

Having said all this, I have to reiterate that significant wealth and a life of joy aren't mutually exclusive. You can have the life you've always wanted and lots of money. You and God would both be pleased with that. The problem is when we think it's the money that will give us the joy we crave. It's not just wealthy people who make this mistake. There are plenty of poor people who have chased the money and missed out on the joy too. At the end of the day, both the rich and the poor run the risk of being exhausted—and regretful—about the time and relationships that slipped away while they chased the next buck.

When Hollywood, Madison Avenue, and Wall Street say to go one way, and your heart says to go the other, it's hard to resist the bright lights and attractive lifestyle. It was very hard for me. It's not that way for everyone, mind you. Plenty of people can follow their hearts and not have to change their current line of work or risk their incomes.

GUT CHECK

For me, I had become convinced at age forty, after much coaching and introspection, that my calling was to help people discover their calling. It was clear to me that I was going to have to leave the corporate consulting game. Helping people discover real purpose and joy is hard when you're a consultant based in Colorado, working with a firm headquartered in San Francisco, managing a virtual team of consultants all over the country, and most of your clients are in the Midwest. I knew I was going to have to leave that platform and that in the short term it would reduce my income.

Fortunately, we had saved well and had a head start on retirement and the kids' college funds. All we needed to do was buckle down on spending and avoid debt at all costs. The first real test that revealed my addiction to other peoples' opinions came when we needed to buy a new car. We decided on a Hyundai. It was a gut check for me the first time I pulled into my friend's driveway for a summer barbecue and everyone else was driving Range

Rovers, BMWs, and Infinitis. I had more than a twinge of self-doubt about the path I had chosen. But you know what—they're just cars, right? Are you going to miss out on the joy God has for you because of a car?

EIGHTEEN INCHES

I recall one specific money issue I wrestled with as I entertained departing from the American Dream playbook. My coach asked me a simple question that rocked my world: "Do you believe you are responsible for your family's financial security?" The answer I knew from Scripture was different from the answer in my Wall Street–hoodwinked brain. My silence on the end of the phone prompted my coach to end our call by gently saying, "Don't feel like you need to answer that now. And don't feel like I'm expecting you to answer a certain way. I do, however, recommend you take some time to noodle on that question."

I was familiar with Jesus saying, "Seek first his kingdom and his righteousness, and all these things will be given to you as well" (Matt. 6:33). The "things" He was referring to were the food, clothing, and shelter His disciples were questioning Him about. I had a big knowing–believing gap here. The eighteen inches between my head and my heart seemed more like twelve feet. I knew that scripture, but did I really, really, *really* deep down inside believe it? The answer to my coach's question came up "yes," I did believe I was responsible for my family's financial security, and I was disappointed in my lack of faith.

What I was doing is something I see a lot of people do. I was trapped in myopic, binary thinking: focus on your peak earning years *or* follow your heart and be broke. I have no idea where that flawed thinking came from, but I knew I had to find a more creative solution.

In my late thirties and early in my Christian walk, Michelle and I were first exposed to the concept of tithing: consistently giving 10 percent of our income back to the local church. I was blown away—actually, shocked —with this idea. What were these people thinking? I had spent my entire adult life investing in ways to *make* 10 percent, not give it away! I was convinced there was an intergenerational church conspiracy going on here.

Michelle and I had the opportunity to speak privately with an older couple whom we respected, and we asked them about this tithing thing. They explained that God wants to give us the desires of our heart and that the desire of His heart is for us to trust Him. Tithing is one way to trust Him. They also explained that the desires of our heart—real joy—are not as connected to our financial prosperity as we think.

This dumbfounded me. My moods before becoming a believer were always directly correlated to my income. If the bank account was healthy, I felt good; if not, I felt lousy. In fact, at that time of life I couldn't imagine anyone using anything *but* money as a primary indicator of happiness. What other metric was there?

The other thing this couple shared in a sincerely humble way was that 10 percent didn't feel sacrificial or faithful to them anymore. Over time, they had increased their giving to 30 percent! And these were not wealthy people giving out of great abundance, mind you.

Michelle and I looked at Malachi 3:10: "'Bring the whole

tithe into the storehouse, that there may be food in my house. Test me in this,' says the LORD Almighty, 'and see if I will not throw open the floodgates of heaven and pour out so much blessing that there will not be room enough to store it.'" The question loomed before us: Do we believe it or not? Is this some metaphor or parable that has to be understood in some ancient cultural context or is it true? Do we try it or ignore this wisdom?

We were learning all of this in November of 2001. My business had become stagnant before the 9/11 collapse. By late November, it was on life support. Now was certainly not the time to start rolling the dice on God to manage our finances. But we were growing in our faith so, when we could least afford to, we wrote our first tithing check.

I hesitate to tell you what happened next because I don't want to be accused of promoting prosperity theology, but the facts are the facts. Within forty-eight hours, I had two job offers with consulting firms both offering me more than I had ever earned. Michelle and I affectionately refer to it as the "Malachi Miracle."

Miracles aside, this impacted me deeply. I didn't get all giddy thinking God was some kind of candy machine, but it did give me confidence that His promises are for real. And sure enough, God has always taken care of 100 percent of our needs and the vast majority of our wants.

WHO OWNS IT?

Christians with significant financial resources have a wonderful generosity challenge: Can you get radically generous—radically trusting—and give lots of that money away? It's not ours in the first place, you know. God gave us the skills, education, connections, good fortune, and work ethic to make that money. Let's boost our joy by seeing how His money can bless others. He may also boost our joy with more money: "Whoever can be trusted with very little can also be trusted with much" (Luke 16:10).

So here are a few rapid-fire recommendations for figuring out where money fits into your joy equation:

1. First and foremost, spend less than you make. The formula for this is amazingly simple: either make more or spend less. Enough said.

2. Look at the concordance of your Bible and read everything it says about money. Even if you don't believe it all yet, you should at least gather the facts about what God has to say on the subject. And He has *a lot* to say about it—mostly warnings.

3. Read Randy Alcorn's *The Treasure Principle*, Ralph Doudera's *Wealth Conundrum*, or anything by Larry Burkett and Ron Blue. These godly men have devoted their lives to teaching the true Christian perspective on money.

4. Create a budget. Many families— especially wealthy ones—don't do this. It is essential that you get some precision—and if you're married, agreement—on your income, savings, and giving. This practice will take some discipline, and the conversations will require some courage.

5. Work at distinguishing between needs and wants. For

example, you need food. Bread, meat, vegetables, eggs—
those are needs. Eating out at a five-star restaurant every
night is a want. Focus more on your needs than your wants.

6. Get your kids involved in some way. Let them know about
the financial decisions you are making and why.

7. Get a friend, an advisor, or a coach to hold you accountable
to your plan. Advice is helpful, but accountability and
encouragement are priceless.

8. Test God. The Bible says that finances are the one place we
can put Him to the test. Find various ways to trust God
with your money and see what happens with your heart.
And with your money.

This last strategy was pivotal in my journey toward trusting God with my money. When I decided to join the staff at the
Halftime Institute, Michelle and I crunched the numbers every
way imaginable. With some real belt tightening we could afford
a 40 percent cut in pay, but the salary the ministry could afford
represented a full 50 percent cut. It just wasn't doable. But then it
struck me: at some point in my coaching of individuals on their
life purpose, I would end up encouraging people to take a financial risk on God. How could I in all good conscience recommend
that someone do that if I had never done it myself? So, like we had
done with the Malachi Miracle earlier, we took the plunge again.

I can remember distinctly the day I came out of my home
office, almost a year after this decision, to share something with
Michelle that I had discovered. I was pulling together some
information for our accountant for what was going to be an interesting tax year. I discovered we ended up $454 ahead of where we

needed to be. God had sent some money-making opportunities to Michelle and me during the year, and He bridged the 10 percent gap for us. While that year was one of the toughest years of adjustment ever, it was also one of the most spiritually dynamic years of my life. God came through. I imagine this is similar to how the Israelites felt when God provided just enough manna for one day and nothing more.

For that one year I had put my focus on serving God and others instead of focusing on and fretting about money. I was slowly releasing the death grip I had on my preprogrammed dream: the unquestioned and hollow American goal of independent wealth. What a freeing place to be!

It is important I say this yet again: Being independently wealthy is not bad. Money is not bad. It's just that money makes a great slave but a horrible master. Look at the story of the rich young ruler (Matt. 19:16–24). The problem wasn't that he was rich. It was that he was hooked on being rich.

Same with the parable of the landowner whom Jesus called a "fool" (Luke 12:13–23). His problem wasn't money. It was that he was going to take his money and live the life our popular culture says we deserve—to "eat, drink, and be merry." Don't misinterpret this and think that Jesus was saying celebration or wealth is frowned upon. The real issue at hand was selfishness, not having money or having fun. The rich fool was not "rich toward God" (v. 21) or, said another way, not generous to God's children who had needs. Jesus called him a fool because his priorities were wrong.

If your priority is joy but you can't seem to grasp it, search your heart to see if money fears are standing in the way.

Remember our tired old coaching question: If time, money, and failure were not obstacles, what would you do with your life? Lean into that question. Journal on it. Talk to your spouse and friends about it. Take some courageous steps to live that life. I don't know whether you'll make $50,000 a year or $5 million a year, but you'll never regret living for joy instead of living for money.

Are you ready to give it a try?

ENGAGEMENT

GET IN THE GAME!

If you have carved out some margin in your life so that you can abide in God's presence and rewire your brain to the truth of the world; if you have used some of that margin to increase your self-awareness about how God uniquely wired you; and if you have resolved in your heart what money means to you, your identity, and God's kingdom, then now is the perfect time to discover and engage in your calling. To get in the game. If done right, this step will help you bridge the gap between the life you always wanted and the life you currently have.

Remember, God's plan isn't just to *save* us so we can go to heaven after we die. Nor is He just intending to *free* us from the False Self. His plan is to *enlist* us in doing His work. His Spirit is intended to forgive us, redeem us, heal us, and get us off the bench and back in the game as His hands and feet to help Him fix our broken world.

The Christian life is about loving others on a daily basis: our families, our friends, our coworkers, and those in our communities. Jesus made this clear when He said, "By this everyone will know that you are my disciples, if you love one another" (John 13:35).

It is both a responsibility and a privilege to help our fellow human beings. It's a responsibility because God has equipped each of us to help others in some physical, emotional, practical, financial, or spiritual way. It's a privilege because when God's Spirit flows through us and out into the world in our unique way, the joy of being exactly who we were created to be is exhilarating.

PASSION

When I speak of engagement, I'm talking about engaging in service to others beyond (and in addition to) day-to-day kindness and pitching in where needed. Beyond and in addition to being a "good guy" or a "sweet woman." Beyond volunteering.

I'm suggesting living a life of all-out love. A life where the forty to sixty hours we have every week between Monday and Friday are pure expressions of both who we are and of God's love. A life where our passions, interests, and paychecks are the equivalent of the highest, most noble, and most leveraged gift we could offer our fellow man. This *is* doable. I've seen it in my life and in the lives of many others. All that's required is the creativity and courage to go do it—and to do it in a way that is obvious to all that God is the loving force powering your human effort.

How this plays out in a person's life in a practical sense will vary. It could entail a bold rethinking about your current role and relationships at work. Or it could be diving into some organization or project you are deeply passionate about that's parallel to your work. Or it may mean leaving the marketplace and going into full-time ministry. In God's sight, no model is holier than the other.

NEW PARADIGMS

I can predict when you will take that first step to engage in the work that represents your life purpose. It'll happen when one of two things occurs: (1) when you realize that the blessings you have are so clearly from God and your gratitude becomes so overflowing that you can't help but pay it forward, or (2) when you truly—deep down in your bones—recognize the emptiness and folly of self-centered living. Lacking either of these perspectives, however, people will always continue to think and act selfishly—which in the long run won't serve them well because they'll lack the joy they thought their selfish thinking would provide in the first place.

People who aren't at either of these stages miss out on what Jesus was referring to when He said, "It is more blessed to give than to receive" (Acts 20:35). They're not only missing out on His promise, they're misunderstanding His words. For these folks, this statement sounds like religious gibberish instead of truth.

It is interesting to me how frequently this scripture is mis-quoted. I often hear it repeated as, "It is *better* to give than receive." Substituting "better" for "blessed" wrongly shifts Jesus' message to a moral lesson instead of the spiritual truth that it is: you will be blessed more by giving than by receiving.

How that blessing plays out is something we never know

beforehand. It may be hidden to others but very real to you—like a new, almost inexplicable sense of peace that overtakes your heart. Or that blessing could reveal itself in tangible ways—like an obvious positive change in your circumstances. Just as we don't know *how* that blessing will manifest itself, nor do we know *when* that blessing will show up. Today? Tomorrow? Twenty years from now? All I know is that I am trusting Jesus on this truth. After all, why wouldn't I? Every time in the past that I have finally surrendered a tiny bit of my agenda to God's truths, it always turns out for the better. And because God's Word is trustworthy and consistent for all, the same blessings will occur in your life when you start to give of yourself as He encourages us.

The other misconception about this scripture is that people limit the meaning of "give" to the giving of money. In fact, Acts 20:35 isn't even about money. If you read the full verse you'll see that it describes the giving as "hard work . . . [to] help the weak." It's about your time and your talents. Personally, I feel more blessed when I invest my time and unique gifts into the lives of others than when I give money. For instance, I've written checks to groups that have gone on mission trips, and I've also gone on those mission trips myself. Which do you think gives me more joy?

FREED UP

God's will for our lives, as we are reminded in Romans 12:2, is perfect, which is why we will be perfectly content when we are living in His will. A lot of Christians talk about "finding God's will," but they make it too complicated, maybe even too spiritual. Ephesians 2:10 tells us we have a mission "prepared in advance for us to do"—for us to engage in.

Intuitively we know that we should be doing *something* to love and serve others, but what exactly we should be doing eludes us. Our tendency is to get overly busy volunteering instead of searching for our calling. Like so many well-intentioned Christians, I initially confused volunteering for calling. I knew that faith was more than just accepting God's unconditional love—I needed to proactively pass that love on to others.

I saw my initial role in God's game plan as helping with the bouncy castle, teaching the Bible to middle schoolers, making coffee, and grilling burgers. All nice and necessary things to do, but they weren't my mission. What is true for many is that they are so busy with nice activities that they have no time to discover and engage in God's unique mission for their lives. Good stuff is crowding out the great stuff God put them on the planet to do.

I had an experience that drives this point home. In 2006, as I was getting more convicted that my calling was to help people discover their calling, I knew I had to step off the elder committee at my church. I explained my intentions to one of the other elders, and he said the most gracious and freeing thing to me: "Jeff, if you really believe that this is the direction God is calling you in, you *have* to step off the board. It would be disobedient not to. Plus, you're robbing someone else of their blessing by taking up their spot on the board." You can't imagine how much that perspective and permission freed me up.

VOLUNTEERING VS. CALLING

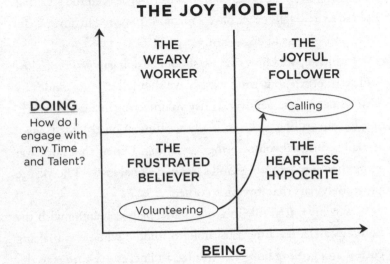

I've discussed the two ways we can proactively love others: one is through humble, selfless, pitch-in-where-needed service, and the other is through our callings, which is the full stewardship of how God has wired us. Both are good for others and good for our souls in their own ways. Let me explain why.

Raw, down-and-dirty, foot-washing volunteer service sometimes just needs to be done. The kids need to get to camp; the tables have to be moved; the coffee has to be brewed; the neighbor's sidewalk needs shoveling; the senior citizen's groceries need carrying. More often than not, the growth, humility, and gratitude we receive from these humble acts of foot-washing volunteerism are their own sufficient reward—even though our initial reaction may be to avoid it.

Richard J. Foster talked about this in his *Celebration of Discipline*:

If true service is to be understood and practiced, it must be distinguished clearly from "self-righteous service."

Self-righteous service comes through human effort. It expends immense amounts of energy calculating and scheming how to render service. Sociological charts and surveys are devised so we can help "those people." True service comes from a relationship with the divine Other deep inside. We serve out of whispered promptings, divine urgings. Energy is expended but it is not the frenetic energy of the flesh. . . . Self-righteous service is impressed with the "big deal." . . . It enjoys serving especially when the service is titanic. True service finds it almost impossible to distinguish the small from the large service. . . .

Self-righteous service requires external rewards. It needs to know that people see and appreciate the effort. It seeks human applause—with proper religious modesty of course. True service rests contented in hiddenness. It does not fear the lights and blare of attention but it does not seek them either. . . .

The flesh whines against service but screams against hidden service. It strains and pulls for honor and recognition. . . .

If we stoutly refuse to give in to this lust of the flesh, we crucify it. Every time we crucify the flesh, we crucify our pride and arrogance.[1]

Humble service is good for our souls.

It's also true that God gave us specific and unique gifts and talents that we shouldn't squander. What would Jesus' ministry look like if He only washed feet and did not mentor, preach, teach, and heal?

So, in addition to selfless volunteerism, we should also be intentional about discerning and engaging in our calling. While it is not a matter of either/or but of both/and, I can tell you that missing out on your true calling leads to missing out on the full joy God has available for you.

"IF ONLY I COULD HEAR GOD'S VOICE"

Any Christ follower's mission in life will always align with what our loving God is trying to do in the big picture of humanity—including reconnecting lost people to Him, redeeming broken lives, restoring an abused earth to perfection, helping the needy and oppressed, and resurrecting our bodies when Jesus comes for the second time. Christians who claim to be living in God's will but aren't doing anything to make things "on earth as it is in heaven" (Matt. 6:10) are fooling themselves.

People often say to me, "If I could only hear God's voice, I swear I would obey Him," meaning they're not sure what God is calling them to do. I remind them that I, too, have never heard an audible voice from God, but that doesn't mean I haven't heard from Him. After all, He's already spoken pretty clearly to us through the Bible. When it comes to what we should be doing for others, there's not much mystery and the list is not all that long:

- Love God and others (Mark 12:30–31).

- Make disciples of all the nations—this refers both to evangelism and discipleship (Matt. 28:19). The first is about encouraging people to believe in Christ. The second is about building up joyful followers of Christ.
- Feed the hungry (Matt. 25:35).
- Give drink to the thirsty (Matt. 25:35).
- Give hospitality and shelter to the stranger/foreigner/ refugee (Matt. 25:35).
- Clothe the naked (Matt. 25:36).
- Care for the sick (Matt. 25:36).
- Visit the imprisoned (Matt. 25:36).
- Help the widows and orphans (Ps. 82:3; Isa. 1:17; and especially James 1:27).
- Provide justice to the oppressed and disenfranchised (Matt. 5:38–45; Mark 10:42–45; Luke 4:18–19).

God has already told us what to do. Our job is to figure out how to use our unique skills, resources, platform, and relationships to impact one or more of those assignments. How do you do that? At the risk of simplifying a process that should be bathed in prayer and usually unfolds over time, here's a step-by-step approach that might help:

1. Apply the skills that give you energy
2. To a cause that makes God *and you* mad, sad, or glad
3. In an organization with the right role and culture for you.
4. Do it all in Jesus' name.

Then you'll be in the flow of what God is trying to do on this earth. Where that all intersects is where your greatest joy in life will be. It won't come from closing another deal, buying your next toy, or checking off your next bucket list item.

The difficulty people have with this list is that they immediately think the only way to obey these commands is to quit their jobs and become the next Mother Teresa. It's important to understand you don't need to go into full-time ministry in order to partner with God on these issues and live more joyfully.

A case could be made that we don't need any more Christians in the nonprofit world. We need more Christians in our schools, banks, factories, department stores, country clubs, movie studios, and hospitals. Everyone can evangelize and disciple (taking an example from the list above) without changing a single thing about their lives—except their paradigm about the people they are already in relationship with.

We all have the option to feed the hungry on weekends or heal the sick during mission trips. We can help fund ministries working on any of these divine assignments without having to sell our companies, quit our jobs, or move to Africa.

I know a CIO (Chief Information Officer) with a passion for eradicating poverty who had had enough of the corporate world. He didn't quit and go to the front lines of serving the least of these. He quit and became the CIO for an organization trying to solve global poverty.

We don't lack clarity from God about what we should be doing. We lack the creativity and courage to go do it.

WHAT NEXT?

So what issue stirs your heart? What cause ignites your passion?

- Inner-city kids with poor education and no positive role models
- The moral decline of our culture
- Health and medicine
- The insularity of the church
- Refugees from war-torn third world countries
- Single moms
- Human trafficking
- Mentoring young married couples
- Building houses for the poor
- Micro-finance in developing nations
- Adoption and foster care
- Legal assistance for migrant workers
- Support for Christian artists, filmmakers, writers
- Outreach to cultures unreached by the gospel
- Interfaith dialogue
- Threats to religious freedom
- Bible translation and distribution

Valid, viable organizations exist to serve each of these areas. And that's just for starters—the list could go on for several pages. Use some of your margin to start paying attention to what's going on in your local, regional, and global community. Make your own list of what fires you up, makes your pulse race. Then ask yourself, "What could I do to bring God's help, hope, and healing to this situation? How could I use the time, talent, and treasure God has given me to make a dent in the problem?"

As you scan your heart and search your soul for your unique mission, pay attention to those moments when tears come to your eyes. What are the scenarios that tug at your heart? A five-year-old in the Ukraine who has spent her entire life in an orphanage? Church planters in India whose homes are being torched by militant Hindus? The young mom ahead of you in the checkout line who has to put some of her groceries back because she doesn't have enough money to pay for them? What's breaking your heart these days?

DON'T FORGET YOUR HOBBIES

It's obvious that we can advance God's kingdom by doing something in addition to our current work. Or we could be God's hands and feet in our place of work. Or we could leave our current work environment and join an organization working on an issue we really care about. But for some people those strategies just aren't the most joyful and leveraged way to live out their calling.

An often overlooked venue for our calling is our hobbies.

I know a Christian businessman named Michael who lived his whole life as a comfortable, obedient Christian: church, reading the Bible, small groups—the whole deal. One day, after listening to a sermon—and reading John Piper's *Don't Waste Your Life*—he felt an overwhelming conviction to get out of his comfort zone and go on a mission trip. But more than that, he needed to bring people with him. The problem is that he had never been on a mission trip himself—let alone led one. What to do? He came up with a creative solution: he had a passion for deep-sea sport fishing, so he decided to use fishing as the lure to get people to go with him to Costa Rica. It worked like a charm. Fourteen men joined him and had a great time big game fishing. Michael also arranged for the fishermen to serve the least of these in villages near their port of call where they were exposed to the darkness of domestic violence, abject squalor, malnutrition, dismal education, and nonexistent health care. These challenges stood in stark contrast to the thirst for the gospel in these communities. Interestingly, the fishermen were blessed as much as the people in the villages. Fast-forward to today and Michael has a ten-person board and five-person staff, and they are leading several trips a year as a strategy to help people grow in their faith and grow in their desire to share their faith (www.reel-life.org). Did I forget to mention that he still has his day job in the insurance industry? Making a living and building the kingdom are not mutually exclusive.

When Michael was a young boy he often went deep-sea fishing with his grandparents and had always dreamed of being a fishing boat captain. He found a creative and courageous way to transform a passion that had the potential to be self-indulgent into a pursuit that is aligned with God's will. It's fishing for men in a whole new way. Talk about joy!

Or consider Mark, who came up to me after a speaking engagement in Orlando, Florida, and said, "I finally figured it out."

"Figured what out?" I asked.

"I know my calling."

He went on to tell me that he and his wife retired to Orlando from Michigan six years prior. He said he had moved so that he could play more golf. All of his Michigan buddies told him he'd be bored with golf within the first twelve months. "But I have to tell you, it's been six years since we moved, and I love golf now more than ever. My handicap is down to two, and I can't get enough of it. But it was starting to seem so self-indulgent. I couldn't reconcile it with my faith. Until one day I realized the other thing I am really passionate about is evangelism. I'm really good at it too. I don't know what it is, but God gave me this unique ability to talk with people about their lives and introduce them to Jesus in an appealing way.

"Instead of always playing golf at my club, I get up three to four mornings every week and call a public golf course and get set up with a threesome of golfers I don't know. My objective at the end of eighteen holes is to have one of those three golfers interested in having a cup of coffee with me to find out more about Jesus."

How cool is that?

My wife, Michelle, took a similar approach. She has been passionate about exercise and nutrition for twenty-five years. Over time, she started to see how many people are frustrated and confused about trying to get healthy. She also noticed that the emotions behind peoples' efforts ranged from helplessness to guilt to pride to shame to vanity. She subsequently scaled back her corporate event planning business and started a global Christian health and fitness ministry that is good for peoples' hearts on multiple levels (www.faithfulworkouts.com). The last eight years of her life have unequivocally been the most joyful of her life. It's no wonder—her love of God, love of people, and love of health and fitness are all completely aligned.

Over the years I have seen people transform their love for hunting, snowboarding, quilting, and car racing into their callings. What are your hobbies? What do you absolutely love to do? How could you use that activity as an organizing principle for getting people together and sharing God's love with them in some creative way? I encourage you to gather up a few friends and brainstorm it for an hour.

START SMALL

Once you sense where God is leading you, it's easy to become so enthused that you go all in. Remember my friend who quickly took the leadership role at a nonprofit only to be fired a year later? That was a "high cost probe." I know of others who jumped at the first opportunity to serve, only to lose enthusiasm, get discouraged, and quit or pull way back. You don't want to get stuck in the upper-left-hand quadrant of the Joy Model (page 32). You can avoid this with "low cost probes"—test-drives and "toe dipping" into issues and causes with measured amounts of time, money, and emotional energy. I'm not recommending you be timid or avoid commitment. I'm suggesting you be discerning.

For example, if God has placed a burden in your heart for the homeless, don't go off and create a new organization aimed at helping the homeless. Instead, volunteer at your local shelter. Serve meals once a week. Hang out for a couple of hours. Get to know the executive director. Ask a lot of questions. All the while asking yourself, "What unique skills or knowledge do I have that would be of value to the homeless?"

Remember, your calling doesn't have to be unpleasant to be

worthy of God. "Suffering for Jesus" is good and healthy as it relates to sacrificial service, but it's not sustainable as a calling. Jesus said we'll always have some level of suffering in our lives, but God gave you your talents and passions so you could joyfully be a part of His larger plan.

MORE MODELS

If you're the kind of person who gets giddy over a spreadsheet and really enjoys budgeting and forecasting, it's probably not a good idea to move to Ethiopia and start building schools. But maybe there are school-building projects in Ethiopia that could use some help with budgets and keeping their finances in order.

In fact, I know a lot of people who do not have a burning passion for any particular cause but just want to use their skills and interests to serve God somehow. I call these folks "cause agnostic." The cause could be clean drinking water, a ministry to AIDS sufferers, or providing Bibles to unreached people groups. It doesn't matter. They simply want to use their skills and knowledge to help others.

For example, a guy who served most of his career as the CFO (Chief Financial Officer) of a major US corporation told me, "I really don't care where I serve as long as Jesus is involved, the people I work with are smart, and the goal of the organization is to help the least of these. I'll make it my mission to be the CFO of any organization that fits those criteria." And why not? There's nothing that says you have to completely reinvent yourself in order to have a fulfilling mission.

And then there are the folks who do in fact reinvent themselves. Accountants becoming artists. Consultants becoming life coaches. Christian-killers becoming Christian-builders. It happens.

Steve was an attorney on Capitol Hill for thirty-two years. Gray suit. White shirt. Red tie. Trudging up the steps every morning. Thirty-two years. When I met him he had moved to Georgia and was excited about his new life. He told me that he now owns a pickup truck.

"Jeff, you don't know me well, but trust me when I say it feels *really* good to say that I actually own a truck," he told me with a chuckle.

Every morning he gets up and throws his tool belt in the back of the truck and goes downtown for breakfast and coffee with some of his buddies. Then they head out to repair the homes of people in the community who can't afford to fix the leaking faucet, replace the wooden steps on the front porch, or patch a hole in the roof. All of this in Jesus' name. As he shared this with me, I could hear the energy and joy building in his voice. It's clear that he's loving life.

Yet another way to find your mission is to bloom where you're planted. Increasingly, companies big and small are looking for ways to give back to their communities. It's called Corporate Social Responsibility, or CSR, and it offers employees various opportunities to serve. This could become your mission or, more likely, a low cost probe to test-drive several different ways to help others.

I worked with one business owner who decided to use his business as a platform for discipling his 175 employees, all his subcontractors, clients, and suppliers—not in a heavy-handed or in-your-face way, but by applying biblical principles to everything they do. His passion is to show a perspective on Christian living that is often distorted by the media or, ironically, misguided Christians. So in everything from hiring practices to relationships with clients to conflict resolution, he and his leadership team model the teachings of Jesus and make it clear that their approach is based on the Bible. His entire career is his mission, which makes going to work every day a source of joy and purpose. And his company is more like a church than a lot of churches I know.

Speaking of churches, most, if not all, of the larger megachurches have created ministries that provide opportunities for the kind of service that will infuse your life with joy and purpose. Perhaps the most visible of these is Saddleback Community Church in southern California. If you go to the church's website, you will see a tab labeled "Act," and it has nothing to do with bouncy castles or making coffee. We're talking major efforts against poverty, disease, illiteracy, etc. At Willow Creek Community Church in the Chicago area, similar opportunities are offered. In fact, many churches are finding a warm welcome from financially depressed city governments. In Detroit, for example, Oak Point Church has a formal relationship with one of the poorest city high schools to provide mentoring services. And in my own state of Colorado, a group of Christian businessmen regularly mentor inner-city students in the public school system, influencing them with the gospel in the process. Church-state issues often evaporate where the needs are greatest. If you attend a larger church, maybe the best first step toward joy would be to spend some time with the pastor in charge of volunteer ministries.

Of course, the simplest way to "bloom where you are planted" is to simply be a blessing to the folks you meet in the everyday rhythms of your life—your spouse, your kids, coworkers, the waitress, the bank teller. This may not constitute your highest calling, but it's the least we can do to share God's love daily.

BE PATIENT

Finding your unique mission takes time. The pattern often looks like this: You test-drive an opportunity that seems like a perfect fit. It's something you're passionate about, is in dire need of your skills and knowledge, and even passes the "fun" test. You could easily see yourself almost jumping in with both feet. Almost. Something just doesn't seem right. Maybe as you explore further you learn that the organization's plans for your involvement are different from your own. Or you sense it's going to take more time and resources than you're able to commit. "Almost" is tempting, but don't settle for it, because in the long run it will become more of an obligation than a source of joy.

Again, I'm not saying be selfish and start thinking that this is all about you. I'm saying be a good steward of your time and talent. Search your heart to know the difference.

In my experience of coaching people through this process, seldom does anyone get it right on their first try. One of the biggest challenges when that first low cost probe doesn't pan out is to resist seeing it as failure. A low cost probe that doesn't work out doesn't mean you aren't spiritual enough for ministry.

There is also the temptation to blame a stalled low cost probe on the organization: "Those ministry guys just don't get it. They don't have a clue about strategy or organizational effectiveness.

They won't listen to common sense." These are not helpful reactions. If your test-drive comes up short, don't think of it as failure. Think of it as another cycle of learning. Have you always bought the first car you drove at the dealership?

My point is that you may need to low cost probe several options before you find the one that fits you best. And it's worth the wait. As long as you continue to give yourself margin and abide with God, He will guide you to the place He has prepared you to serve: "Trust in the LORD with all your heart and lean not on your own understanding; in all your ways submit to him, and he will make your paths straight" (Prov. 3:5–6).

It may seem like a simple illustration, but just as healthy apple trees produce apples, healthy Christians produce fruit in the form of lives transformed by God's love.

But before you get overly focused on serving the needs of "the least of these," remember there are people already in your life who need you.

RELATIONSHIPS

YOUR RICHEST GIFTS

The great nineteenth-century preacher C. H. Spurgeon once said, "Discernment is not knowing the difference between right and wrong. It's knowing the difference between right and almost right."

Isn't that often the challenge we face with most decisions— knowing the best course of action when the options we must choose from are all good in different ways? Every choice we make is by default a choice not to do something else. And discernment doesn't only kick in during major life decisions—it comes into play several times each day.

Such is the case when it comes to relationships. How much time should I dedicate to which relationships? How do I balance love with truth? What's the right way to handle different situations? All of these decisions have a huge impact on the quality of our lives, our relationships, and our joy.

In fact, I would say that poorly managed and neglected relationships are far and away the most common reason for self-inflicted pain in peoples' lives. Note that I said self-inflicted. Much of the stress in peoples' lives comes from relational issues that could be completely avoided.

I'm addressing relationships last in this book only because it comes last in my M.A.S.T.E.R. Plan acrostic. While every element in this plan is vitally important to your joy, your relationships may be the most important factor in determining your joy. (Second to your relationship with God, of course.) You may find and engage in your calling, but if you neglect your family and friends, you're inviting stress and heartbreak into your life.

FAMILY MAN, CAREER GUY

For many people, especially men who are professionals, the time challenges they wrestle with in their careers take a huge toll on their wives and kids. Long, irregular hours and travel are the usual suspects. There is no mystery here. No deep theological or spiritual insight is required. Clearly, less time with those closest to you leads to shallow relationships—the antithesis of the deep, fun, and intimate relationships we all want.

I remember leading a workshop once and asking a gentleman during a break why he decided to attend. He told me he had created a revolutionary knee brace for athletes and spent the last five years of his life traveling to woo investors, meet with doctors, and talk with professional sports teams. The week prior to the workshop he was actually at home one weekday morning. He was eating breakfast by himself in his kitchen before his wife and eight-year-old daughter were awake. There on the refrigerator door was a hand-colored picture of a stick-figure mom holding hands with a stick-figure little girl. The title of the picture was "My Family." He had to get to the office before his daughter woke up, so he couldn't ask her about it. But that picture haunted him all day. He made it home that night in time for dinner and asked his daughter about the drawing. "Why aren't I in the picture, honey?" She said, as nonchalantly as you could imagine, "Aw, Dad. You're never around." And she went back to eating her peas. Ouch.

As one of my coaching friends likes to say to his hard-charging, workaholic clients: "What's all your winning actually costing you?" Take a moment right now to move that question from the rhetorical to the personal. What toll is your work taking on your life? Your family? Your friendships? Your health?

At a very basic level, just being physically present is half the battle. The other half is being mentally present while your body is in the same room! It's not an easy thing to do. Even when the smartphone isn't ringing or beeping, there is this incredible urge to sneak a peek. I know this firsthand. What's behind that? Fear of missing out on something? Fear of letting someone down? Fear of sending the signal that we're not as committed to the team as the rest of our workaholic coworkers?

Now flip the coin over and ask, what's the message we're sending to our kids, spouse, and friends when we're mentally and emotionally absent? When we're having conversations with them but our eyes never leave the phone, computer screen, or TV?

So how do these dynamics impact our joy? The long-term effect of infrequent, transactional, and superficial relationships with your spouse and kids is that you won't build intimacy, honesty, and trust. And then, when your spouse or children really need you—or you need them—there is no precedent for sharing and authentic communication. They turn to other sources for that.

A friend of mine told me that his forty-year-old office mate described how his father was a "good dad, a provider, but was never there for me when I was growing up and needed him most." My friend had always noticed an undercurrent of anger in his office mate. This information filled in the pieces of the puzzle.

If we had a crystal clear picture of what we want our most important relationships to look like twenty years from now, we might have more motivation to be more strategic about how we treat those closest to us. Or, conversely, if we had a sense of what a life twenty years from now with obliterated relationships would be like, we'd be motivated to make some positive changes right now.

A GOOD THING GONE BAD

The opposite of not having enough time for our families is that we spend too much time doting on them—or too much money spoiling them. This is especially true with our children. Making our kids the center of our lives sends the signal to them that life is all about them. The message we are unintentionally searing into their brains is that parents are supposed to work hard and then use the rest of their time and money treating their kids like royalty. If we continue down this path, they'll never witness true

Christian living where we care for our families *and* serve others outside of our families.

This problem is rampant in our culture in general. I read of a superintendent of schools who was nominated as Public Education Administrator of the Year in his state. He had the honor of addressing his peers in an auditorium at the largest high school in the state. Before he took the stage, he had to go to the bathroom. Above the mirrors was a giant sign that said, "You are looking at a very special person." At that moment, he tossed his prepared speech in the wastebasket and changed his presentation. He made the case to change that mantra above the mirror to "What nice thing have you done for someone today?"

Healthy self-esteem is valuable, but chronic self-centeredness is toxic.

It's all about discernment—knowing the subtle difference between nurturing your children and spoiling them. Or the difference between modeling service outside of the family and neglecting your family. I encourage you to frequently get real honest with yourself and do a personal assessment regarding this balancing act. Then have the courage to make the necessary adjustments.

Our relationships extend beyond our families, of course. What about our friends and coworkers in our social circles? Are we making time for those people? If so, are we making time because we want something from them or because of what we can give to them? Selfless or selfish?

The angst we experience from broken relationships can sometimes be traced to the lack of time invested in those relationships. Other times it can be traced to wrong motives and attitudes toward those relationships. Some folks have a disastrous habit of using people and loving things—instead of the other way around. Where is your heart?

THE HEART OF RELATIONSHIPS

I remember my first Christian men's retreat. I didn't know the real Jesus then, but I was promised we'd have some time to fly-fish, so I went. Personally, I was a little creeped out—a bunch of grown men holding hands and praying in a parking lot before we jumped in cars and headed to the mountain retreat center. Community bromance.

When we entered the conference center, our pastor had placed a Bible, a twenty-dollar bill, and a modest, framed picture of a woman on the entryway table.

We spent the weekend discussing the right way to prioritize those three things. I was convinced it went money, then my wife, then God. It just made sense to me: focus on work so you can provide for your wife and then weave a little God into the mix with the time left over. What's so complicated about that? What could possibly be wrong with it?

Our pastor suggested the order be (1) God, (2) your wife, and (3) work. I was dumbfounded. (Remember the upside-down kingdom of God?) He said the best thing you could do for your wife and your career is to get fully acquainted with the true nature and character of God and how He set up the world to function. He contended that if we did that our wives would notice the difference and be forever grateful.

I didn't walk away from that weekend with some amazing

epiphany or massive change in thinking. I was sticking to my guns. But something started to happen to Michelle that did change my mind.

I noticed that she was reading the Bible a lot. I also started to see some changes in her behavior. I didn't know if it was spiritual fruit growing in her or her willingness to put common sense from the Bible into action (in retrospect, it was undoubtedly both), but she was changing. Her heart was changing. Our relationship was changing.

You see, Michelle and I are both pretty strong willed. Probably she is more than I am. No condemnation here. Just the truth. She'd agree. If you know anything about the StrengthsFinder assessment, her top three strengths are Belief, Command, and Self-Assurance. Early in our marriage we used to really butt heads over various issues. As she started to read the Bible more and listen to sermons online, I could see her start to back down on differences of opinion when things started to heat up. It was so obvious to me. She was changing before my eyes over the course of six to twelve months. She wasn't avoiding conflict or denying her emotions. She was simply becoming more loving and discerning about when to stop fighting a particular battle in order to win the more important war of building a thriving marriage.

Not to be outdone, I decided I needed to loosen up a bit and not be so stubborn—especially on the smaller issues of life. There's truth to the saying "you can catch more flies with honey than with vinegar." I think that's the everyday version of "Do unto others as you would have them do unto you."

The next thing I knew, we were in a nice-fest. A competition about who could be nicer. Of course, she trounced me in that competition. Always has. Always will. She's just a more giving person than I am. That's the truth—not false humility. She's proof that you can be strong willed and very loving.

Putting God first changed her heart. More compassionate. More discerning about when to dig in and when to let it go. More sensitive to how others are viewing a situation. More Christ-like.

Do we still have some arguments? You bet. There are major decisions we need to make that we sometimes disagree on. The good thing is that the disagreements are less frequent and more civil.

Our relationship improved because our hearts were changing. Our hearts were changing because we were both abiding with Christ more and experiencing the spiritual fruit of love. When you abide with Christ for an extended period of time, you'll notice that you don't have to grit your teeth and try to be loving. You will naturally become more loving (and lovable). And joy shows up.

Think about Ron, the pharmaceutical guy we discussed in chapter 6, and his battle with selfish ambition. I know that his direct reports are thriving under his leadership now that he has identified his heart issue and is letting God rinse it out of his soul. It's not only good for his employees, but he lives freer and more generously. He gets a kick out of helping people grow and advance in their careers instead of being in a stressful competition to outshine them.

I battle with these heart issues that are detrimental to relationships too. I once took a self-assessment that said, "Jeff has a propensity toward self-promotion." That struck a nerve. I know there are times when I will artfully make a comment that has the most subtle way of bragging. Even if the people I am interacting with don't notice it, I do. And it bothers me. There's something in my heart that craves recognition. I pray often for God to release me from that.

Truth be told, I know what it is in my heart that craves that recognition. It's the dark side of my "love language," which is Words of Affirmation. The love language concept comes from Gary Chapman's book *The Five Love Languages*. His research and counseling experience revealed that people have preferences for how they feel most loved by others. Words of Affirmation. Quality Time. Acts of Service. Physical Touch. Receiving Gifts.

Much like the StrengthsFinder, knowing our love language is helpful in building self-awareness and managing healthy relationships. (I strongly recommend you and everyone in your family do both assessments and talk through them.) However, make note, every strength and love language that is overused or misapplied can backfire on us.

Be brutally honest with yourself about the heart issues (ego, pride, fear, insecurity, greed) that are deteriorating your relationships. Self-deception about what really drives your thinking and interpersonal interactions will hold you back. Your relationships and life will never be all you want if you can't get real with yourself. Self-authenticity is an unequivocal prerequisite to growth and joy.

CULTIVATING HEALTHY RELATIONSHIPS

I am not a marriage counselor or family therapist. Instead, like all good coaches, I help people identify the issues that are negatively impacting their lives, help them create strategies and find resources for making adjustments, and then help them stay accountable to their goals and commitments.

An excellent coach needs to be a subject matter expert in only one area in order to effectively help a person live a more joyful life—that is true coaching.

Having said that, I do have some experience in—and a huge appreciation for—the skill of effective communication. In my years as a leadership development consultant, I had the privilege of exposure to the latest writing, teaching, and research on how to communicate well.

The old saying that "communication is not what is said, but what is heard" is absolutely true.

Even if people are committed to making time for their key relationships and have their hearts in the right place, they can torpedo relationships with the wrong word choice, inappropriate tone, bad timing, or offensive body language.

The proverb, "The tongue has the power of life and death, and those who love it will eat its fruit" (Prov. 18:21), reveals the result of good and bad communication styles. If you use the tongue in a mean-spirited way, you will eat the fruit of miserable relationships. If you use it to give life and love, you will eat the fruit of healthy relationships.

Unfortunately, many people try to speak life and love, but the words just don't come out right. One of the most common communication mistakes that I see sucking the joy out of peoples' relationships has to do with conflict resolution. Conflict is unavoidable. It will happen to everyone in any truly authentic relationship. Handling it well will build high-trust, low-stress relationships. The most obvious unhealthy way to deal with conflict is to avoid it. Bad strategy.

The steps to healthy conflict resolution between two adults are fourfold:

1. Speak only about specific, observable, and undeniable facts about the situation.
2. Share how you feel about the situation or what the person did. No one can deny how you feel about the situation or what actually occurred.
3. Never make an inference about *why* a person did something or what their motivation was for acting a certain way.
4. Ask them to clarify their view of the situation and what they suggest should be done moving forward.

Bad example: "Bob, this is the third time this quarter that you've submitted budget numbers that are completely messed up. It makes me think you don't see this as an important part of running this business. Something has to change ASAP."

Good example: "Bob, this is the third time this quarter that you've submitted budget numbers that are not adding up or are missing key data. It's really messing up my ability to forecast for the whole company. What's going on and how can I help you get them done right?"

Bad example: "Honey, the way you constantly badger me about all these issues is driving me crazy. Why can't you just trust me and know that I'm doing the best I can to figure things out?"

Good example: "Honey, when you continually revisit the same issues we've already resolved, it really frustrates me. What can we do to create a plan, agree to it, and start making the situation better?"

Most people I know see the value in this approach and can get good at starting conversations using this technique. The challenge is keeping your cool and finding the right words when the other person isn't playing nice and he or she retorts to your opening comment with venom. My advice here is to acknowledge the emotion ("I can see you're bothered by this and I feel bad that you feel that way") and go back to the formula:

1. Clarify the original—and any new—facts that have been revealed.
2. Share how it is impacting you and that you'd like to improve the situation for both of you.
3. Make no inference about why the other person is saying something or why he or she did something.
4. Ask the person to clarify the renewed perspective on the situation and how he or she thinks you should move forward.

You may need several cycles of this communication structure until you can come to an agreement. Not only will this strategy de-escalate these contentious conversations, but you are building trust with the other person, which will minimize the emotional load of future disagreements.

Now, some people may read this and think, *I'm not going to get all mealymouthed here and start dancing around the real issues. If I have an opinion and feelings to share, I'm going to share them.*

To that I say, "Be my guest . . . and enjoy the fruit that approach produces. You reap what you sow."

Relationships are hard. They take time. Conflict happens, and we too easily revert back to our win-lose approaches rather than win-win. But the time and effort you put into your relationships will contribute to the joy and fulfillment in your life. Throughout this book I have frequently advised that you get some help—that you shouldn't make this critical journey alone. When it comes to relationships, that advice is even more critical. The couple who agrees to some outside help is not acknowledging failure but preserving success.

———

Joy and fulfillment. That's been the goal throughout this book. A lot of people begin to make the changes necessary to attain joy only to get stuck.

It doesn't have to happen to you.

ELEVEN

DON'T TRY THIS ALONE

You would think that with all wonderful books, programs, and ministries available to Christians, we wouldn't have so many believers who are just barely hanging on and wrestling with smoldering discontent.

For example, one of my favorite books that speaks to our hunger for purpose and meaning is *The Purpose Driven Life* by Rick Warren. I love this book. And so did 30 million other readers. When my small group went through this book many years ago, we got all fired up, but nothing significant or lasting changed for any of us. I know that millions have been radically transformed by this book, but I also know that many more have had the same experience we did. Why? I think the answer is because we underestimate the challenge of the knowing-doing gap: the disconnect between knowing what to do and actually following through with it. The reason this gap exists is because the challenge at both spiritual and practical levels is underestimated and the realities of our current life get in the way of our future good intentions.

As I interact with Christian life coaches from all over the world who have watched this same phenomenon, it's actually pretty clear why so many people start out strong but fade over time. Here are the usual suspects:

FEAR. This is a broad, all-encompassing sentiment we hear from people. Often they can't really pinpoint what they're afraid of. They simply become "frozen on the trigger," unable and, perhaps subconsciously, unwilling to make any courageous or significant changes in their lives.

NO ACCOUNTABILITY. The transition to a God-honoring, people-loving, joyful life requires courage and action *over an extended period of time.* Rarely is the job finished with one bold, gutsy move. There are multiple decisions to make along the way. If you don't have a person, or group of people, holding you accountable to these steps over a sustained period of time, your odds of reaching your goals are pretty slim.

NO PROVEN, TRUSTED PROCESS TO FOLLOW. Most people need a clearly defined process or plan to keep them going. The most effective and seasoned Christian life coaches I know all have a structured and tested process to help people move forward in their lives.

UNABLE TO HEAR GOD'S VOICE. Many people have a low confidence level about their purpose in life. Even if they have a mission statement, they wonder if it's just their human guess at what would be a "nice life to live." With a low level of conviction about which direction to go with their life, people lack the emotional horsepower to start taking action. This lack of conviction about God's voice in the equation causes hesitancy and self-doubt. Formidable challenges, indeed. But remember, joy shouldn't be the focal point of our lives. Otherwise we'll never attain it. Joy is the *by-product* of aligning ourselves with God's will and serving others.

MONEY WORRIES. When people initially consider pursuing their biggest dreams and true life purpose, many assume their income and net worth must decrease. The fact is that when people decide to wholeheartedly pursue a life of loving God and others, some peoples' net worth will decrease, but others will surely increase.

EGO AND IDENTITY. Experiencing a significant life change means by default that I will be less like I have been in my past. This is frightening to us because we have invested so much time and energy to become who we are today. Our titles, roles, social circles, and peoples' opinions of us may change, and the question of who we really are looms big.

UNSUPPORTIVE FRIENDS AND FAMILY. When people commit to discovering the joy of truly following Jesus, many of their friends and family often think they are being irresponsible, going off the deep end, taking things a little too far, or putting their families at risk. This worldly thinking from friends and family creates a massive psychological headwind.

NORMS OF THE POPULAR CULTURE. The daily barrage of messages from a culture steeped in consumerism, relativism, selfishness, and crude humor is completely counter to our attempts to tap into our greatest peace and joy. Swimming against this current is a significant obstacle for many.

BUSYNESS. The hectic pace of daily living can be a serious impediment because it crowds out the time to thoughtfully and prayerfully strategize about our lives. Getting to know how God has wired us and where, specifically, we fit into His plan takes time. There are no two ways about it: you will need to stop doing something in order to start intentionally sorting through your next season of life.

IT SHOULDN'T BE SO DIFFICULT

As I was working on this final chapter, I heard my favorite Scottish pastor, Alistair Begg, say this on his radio program: "Hearing plus obeying equals blessing."[1] My heart leapt. That's exactly how we find the joy and fulfillment we've been missing. In fact, that's the whole thesis of this book and the Joy Model: "Being plus Doing equals Joy."

It really *can* be this easy. I've seen people get serious about their lives, start paying attention to sermons, read the Bible more diligently, cultivate hearts of humility and gratitude, get in community with other believers and encouragers, and start making bold changes in their lives to love God and others more effectively. God is certainly capable of enabling that kind of change, and my hunch is that you've seen it happen to others too.

Unfortunately, I have also seen way more people get serious about changing their lives and try to make the necessary adjustments only to get stalled and dragged back into the status quo. As the old saying goes: "When all is said and done, more is often said than done."

So how do you proceed without getting stuck? There are a few options to choose from:

Do It Yourself

Given the obstacles I listed above, the "do it yourself" approach may seem unwise. And, in my opinion, it is. But it is the typical default strategy for many people, especially men. I did it this way for a few years but made little progress.

Going solo works for some people, but not many.

We are not only designed to live in community, but our fullest potential in life emerges in community: "Iron sharpens iron" (Prov. 27:17). "A cord of three strands is not quickly broken" (Eccl. 4:12). "Where two or three gather in my name, there am I with them" (Matt. 18:20).

Isolation usually leads to self-deception and bad decisions. One of the reasons for this is that the human mind has an incredible capacity for rationalizing things. "I'll get to it later." "That goal is not as critical as I thought it was when I started this journey." "Maybe things aren't so bad after all." "Maybe I don't need to be so drastic."

The problem with this rationalizing is that it causes us to stuff the feelings of discontent down into our hearts for a while, and we lose the momentum and inspiration that got us going in the first place. But, inevitably, those feelings will flare up again at a later date, and we find ourselves wrestling with the same issues that plagued us when we started. And now we're no closer toward making the hard changes that we knew we needed to make way back then. And the clock keeps ticking. Some people get trapped in this cycle for years—even their whole lives.

Going solo has worked for some, but it is the least effective option.

Small Groups

Going through the M.A.S.T.E.R. Plan described in this book with a small group can make a huge difference both in terms of spiritual growth (Being) and the practical application of what you are learning (Doing). Small groups seem to be the preferred option for growth today in the American church, and it's a particularly effective strategy for getting people from large churches into smaller groups to learn together and to "do life" together.

Small groups are designed to be places where the hurting, confused, and lonely can come to receive God's love, healing, encouragement, and acceptance.

Small groups are also helpful in getting people together to study the Bible or books about living with the Holy Spirit. Having a venue where people schedule time to read, study, and discuss issues is incredibly helpful for motivating, edifying, and keeping us accountable to read and get more of the right information in our brains.

Having people to kick ideas around with is a huge bonus too.

I know this was instrumental to the growth of my faith early on. Having five or six couples discuss a Bible verse, read the study notes, go back and forth on what it meant to us, and then discuss how it applied to our lives was great. And there is enormous power and comfort in being able to share our struggles, celebrate our victories, hold ourselves accountable, and do fun stuff with a group of people who care about us and share our values.

If you decide to work on your Being and Doing via the small group strategy, here are a few cautions and recommendations:

LEADERSHIP. Sometimes a small group is essentially "the blind leading the blind." Make sure the person who leads your group has had some real-life experience in both the Being and Doing categories. This person should be a mature believer who also has a clearly defined calling embodied in service to others. Do you see him or her living a life of Holy Spirit–empowered joy that is attractive to you?

SIZE AND TIME. Most small groups comprise seven to fourteen members and meet every one to four weeks for an hour or two. It's a design that works well for people to learn Scripture, but it doesn't enable individuals to go deep with the specifics of their challenges and goals on the Doing and Being dimensions. Typically what happens is that one person dominates the discussion or everyone ends up being forced to stay at a superficial level because of time constraints. A smaller group of three or four people would be much more helpful because it allows enough time for everyone to dig deeply into the process of change.

ACCOUNTABILITY. Holding people accountable can get weird sometimes. There are times when people say they want to be held accountable but don't really mean it. They simply say it because they feel pressured to. And then they get all touchy when someone asks how it's going. It's important that everyone in your group is clear on what accountability means. Accountability done well is when a person is asked how things are going with the goals that person previously committed to. And then, if he or she has fallen short, the person receives brainstorming, advice, and encouragement. Not condemnation or judgment. Problems bubble up when the person receiving the input is thin-skinned and doesn't truly want to change or confront challenges. It also gets unhealthy when the people giving feedback mask judgment in the cloak of "truth-telling in love."

Mentoring

A mentor is a mature individual who spends time sharing his or her experience, love, guidance, and wisdom with someone less mature. In many circumstances, it can be a powerful strategy for personal and spiritual growth.

If you choose the mentoring route, make sure your focus is to grow into the person God designed you to be rather than trying to become like your mentor. An effective mentor provides guidance more by asking provocative and insightful questions than by simply telling you what to do. Great mentors are more concerned with what you want to accomplish rather than what they want you to accomplish. To that end, you need to be explicit about what you hope to gain through your mentor. For instance, "I need specific help with my faith (or career or finances or marriage, etc.)."

Coaching

If it appears that I'm spending more time on coaching than the other options, you're right. And for good reason. In my experience, both as a coach and as someone who has benefited from being coached, it's the surest way to achieve your goals of joy and fulfillment. Many people I have talked to over the years about coaching have asked why I feel going solo, small groups, and mentoring—all proven methods of personal growth throughout the history of Christianity—aren't viable strategies for helping people move from Frustrated Believers to Joyful Followers. Why does it have to be coaching? My response is always the same: those *are* viable strategies for growth, but they don't work for everyone. Some people need and want a different approach to growth. And coaching is one such approach that I think many people are unfamiliar with, but need to know about.

When I recommend coaching to friends or colleagues, however, I sometimes get that "deer in the headlights" look. To them, coaching and joy do not belong on the same playing field—that is, until I explain what coaching is all about.

The first confusion I encounter comes from what most people think of when they hear the word *coach*. One of two images come to mind: the beloved sports coach who taught them, loved them unconditionally, and challenged them to achieve more than they thought they ever could; or the emotionally stunted Neanderthal who, while frustrated with his own high school athletic career, decided to spend his adult life berating and belittling kids under the guise of "sports is such a great analogy for life."

When I use the word *coach*, I am not talking about either of those models.

The word *coach*, as it relates to facilitating growth in someone, comes from the old English concept of transportation—like a horse-drawn "stagecoach" or the coach that Cinderella rode in. A coach is a means for getting people from point A to point B.

Certainly athletic coaches can play this role, but the real distinction I am using with the word *coach* is not just *what* coaches are doing but *how* they are helping a person grow. Athletic coaches use—among other things—love, intimidation, inspiration, expertise, competition, fear, and encouragement to help a person make progress. A true life coach uses—at a high level—love, questions, and self-discovery. The best ones use these skills not only to help people move from point A to point B but to help them understand the reality of their point A, define specifically what they want point B to look like, and then build and execute on a plan for moving forward.

This is what Jesus did. He was the best coach in the world. In addition to telling people the truth in love, we see Him telling stories that leave the listener hanging with unasked questions: "So, what do you think about that?" "So, how does that apply to your life?" "What do you think you should do now?" Jesus let people draw their own conclusions. We don't see Jesus running after the dejected rich young ruler trying to convince him to follow Him or lowering His standards for entering the kingdom so He wouldn't lose the sale. He pointed people to the truth, but let people decide what to do about it.

A second confusion around the kind of coaching I am talking about comes from how the word *coach* is used in the business world today. Most people interpret this adult-to-adult partnership as "personal consulting and accountability." In other words, people think a business coach is hired to assess their professional situation, give them some ideas and recommendations, and then hold them accountable to execute them. There is actually a lot of value in this approach. Good stuff can get done. But often the ownership and excitement for results is undermined because the ideas were imposed on the person, not self-generated. There is a difference between consulting and coaching. A good coach doesn't give you all the answers. He or she asks you all the right questions.

In twenty years of consulting and leadership development in the corporate world, I learned that people don't learn best using the typical approach to education: "I have information. I will share it with you. You regurgitate it back to me. Now go use it." People have greater buy-in to plans that they create themselves than to plans that are assigned to them. Not only that, but the plans they create are often more successful because they know the subtleties of their challenges better than any consultant ever would.

A third misconception about coaching arises when coaching is described as *life* coaching. For some reason, people think life coaching is "counseling lite." Life coaching is not counseling. Counseling is about looking backward, making sense of our past, understanding how the past influences our thinking now, leveraging what is good from our past and trying to heal from what is debilitating. It is this last piece—healing—that so many people desperately need. Counseling provides therapy to help people heal from the pain of their past and enable them to move forward. Coaching is not specifically designed to do this—although when coaching is done through a Christian lens, the Holy Spirit can certainly heal people. More on that in a bit.

Coaching is distinct in that it neither ignores nor attempts to heal the pain from the past, but instead equips people to learn from their past and move forward. As my dad used to say as a football coach to his players: "Are you hurt or are you injured?" There's a difference. And a different course of action is necessary. A life coach's goal is not to bury the pain, but to help you learn from the pain. Just as importantly, life coaches can help their clients determine if they need counseling or not.

Life coaching leverages love, questions, and self-discovery tools and strategies to help people understand their lives, build their self-awareness, create goals, evaluate alternative strategies, stay motivated, and stay accountable to executing on those strategies.

CHRISTIAN LIFE COACHING

Psychologist Gary Collins wrote about the concept of Christian life coaching through his landmark book *Christian Coaching*. He defines Christian life coaching as "the art and science of enabling individuals and groups to move from where they are to where God wants them to be."[2]

My own definition, nuanced over the years and maybe a bit wordy, is "a Christ-focused, Spirit-infused self-discovery process to help people hear from God and get their life 'in alignment with their assignment.'"

Chris McCluskey, another pioneer in the field of Christian

life coaching, has done much to elevate the art and practice of the Christian coaching industry. Chris and his team at the Professional Christian Coaching Institute have been training life coaches all over the world to cultivate the heart, mind, and skills necessary to coach well. Perhaps more important for you to know is that he and his organization have created www.christian lifecoaching.com, a web-based directory for people seeking Christian life coaches to find the right coach for them. Other options for finding a Christian life coach include: www.christian coaches.com, www.youronedegree.com, and www.sdiworld.org. The Halftime Institute (www.halftime.org) also provides coaching to a unique niche: successful people in midlife transition seeking to discover and embrace God's calling on their second half of life.

Choosing the right coach requires some homework. Start with these questions:

1. Do you want a male or female coach?
2. Is there a certain age range that you prefer in a coach?
3. Do you want your prospective coach to have a specific business or nonprofit background?
4. Do you have a specific objective or "problem" you are trying to tackle? You'll find that some coaches have niche practices to help you build margin, abide in Christ, enhance self-awareness, manage your treasure, engage in service or career options, or enhance your relationships. Other coaches are generalists in all these areas, but experts in the broader objective of helping people live more joyfully. Your coach does not need to be an expert in your "problem" for you to get value from his or her coaching expertise.

5. What denomination—if any—would you prefer your coach to be affiliated with?

6. What's been the spiritual journey of your coach and how did he or she get into the coaching profession?

7. What training and experience does this coach have?

8. Can you speak with some of the coach's past or current clients?

9. What's your budget? While every Christian coach I know sees this as their calling and personal ministry, they are also professionals who will charge a fee for their services.

10. Will you prefer phone or face-to-face coaching? Several coaches I know say they are more effective over the phone because they can concentrate and take notes better than when they are face-to-face. My busy clients prefer phone coaching because it saves on drive time and other associated costs.

WHAT'S THE VALUE PROPOSITION?

A good Christian life coach helps people:

- Get honest with themselves and make sense of where they are in life right now
- Build their self-awareness about habits and patterns that serve them well and not so well
- Establish short- and long-term goals
- Create viable strategies for moving forward while being cognizant of potential obstacles

- Tap into their own motivations and into the Holy Spirit and Scripture for inspiration
- Stay on track and accountable to their vision
- Remember that Scripture is the ultimate filter for decision making

It's this unique mix of help that makes me such a fan of Christian life coaching. At the end of the day, however, no one but you can do the work that's required to move you up and to the right on the Joy Model—that place where your faith and your day-to-day living integrate into the life of joy that you dream about.

So lean into God and then live and love out of who you are becoming. It's the vine and the branch. Abiding and obeying. The spiritual and the practical. It is being exactly who God created you to be, walking in His presence, doing what you do best, what you enjoy, for God and others.

The frustrations you are feeling will be transformed into joy, fulfillment, purpose. But remember, those are the benefits, not the goal. The goal is to be a conduit for God's love and to give Him the glory.

"For whoever wants to save their life will lose it, but whoever loses their life for me and for the gospel will save it. What good is it for someone to gain the whole world, yet forfeit their soul?" (Mark 8:35–36).

When you give in Christ's name, you gain. When you obey and submit to God, you experience freedom. It's the upside-down kingdom inviting you to the adventure of your life. Hold on tight and enjoy the ride.

ACKNOWLEDGMENTS

First and foremost, I need to thank Bob Buford. His life has inspired me. His book *Halftime* gave me permission to dream again. His organization (the Halftime Institute) and his generosity made this book materialize.

Thank you to my coaches, Greg Murtha and Dave Jewitt, who had my best interests at heart and challenged me to keep leaning into Jesus . . . trusting that joy and a sense of purpose would be the outcome.

To the Board of Directors and all of my teammates at the Halftime Institute who gave me the encouragement and gift of time to write this book.

To my mom and dad: After hearing the life stories of so many people I have coached over the years, I will never take your unconditional love and patience for granted. It's a blessing to be your son.

To God: I am so thankful that He gave us the written Word to make sense of our lives.

ABOUT THE AUTHOR

Jeff Spadafora is Director of the Halftime Institute's Global Coaching Services and Product Development (www.halftime.org), where he trains and manages the global Halftime Coaching staff. Earlier, Spadafora was a management consultant for twenty years with a focus on executive education and development for Fortune 500 companies. He lives with his family in Evergreen, Colorado.

NOTES

Chapter 3: Frustration Revealed

1. For more information on this study, check out Greg L. Hawkins and Cally Parkinson's *Move: What 1,000 Churches Reveal about Spiritual Growth* (Grand Rapids, MI: Zondervan, 2011).

2. Hartford Institute for Religion Research, "Fast Facts About American Religion," accessed February 10, 2016, http://hirr .hartsem.edu/research/fastfacts/fast_facts.html#numcong.

3. Brad Waggoner, "Why Adults Switch Churches," LifeWay, accessed February 10, 2016, http://www.lifeway.com/Article /Viewpoint-adults-who-switch-churches.

Chapter 4: What's Wrong?

1. "Lord, I Want to Be a Christian," *Folk Songs of the American Negro*, ed. Fredrick Work and John W. Work Jr. (Nashville, TN: Work Brothers, 1907).

2. Frances R. Havergal, "Take My Life, and Let It Be," Hymnary .org, accessed March 10, 2016, http://www.hymnary.org/text /take_my_life_and_let_it_be.

3. David Van Biema, "Mother Teresa's Crisis of Faith," Time.com, August 23, 2007, accessed March 10, 2016, http://time.com /4126238/mother-teresas-crisis-of-faith/.

Chapter 5: Margin: Making Room for Change

1. HarrisInteractive, "Leisure Time Plummets 20% in 2008—Hits New Low," TheHarrisPoll.com, December 4, 2008, accessed March 10, 2016, http://media.theharrispoll.com /documents/Harris-Interactive-Poll-Research-Time-and -Leisure-2008–12.pdf.
2. Darlinton Omeh, "Top 10 Richest People of All Time in History," Constative.com, July 12, 2013, accessed March 11, 2016, https://constative.com/history/top-10-richest -men-of-all-time-in.

Chapter 6: Abiding: Life with the Spirit

1. "Research," BacktotheBible.org, last updated 2016, accessed March 20, 2016, https://www.backtothebible.org/research.

Chapter 7: Self-Awareness: Who Are You Really?

1. Ed Laymance, "I Am a Child of the King," http://storage .cloversites.com/impactcounselingandguidancecenter /documents/Child%20of%20the%20King.pdf.
2. Bronnie Ware, *The Top Five Regrets of the Dying: A Life Transformed by the Dearly Departing* (Carlsbad, CA: Hay House, 2012).

Chapter 8: Treasure: The Green Monster

1. Angus Deaton and Daniel Kahneman, "High Income Improves Evaluation of Life but Not Emotional Well-Being,"

PNAS.org, 2010, accessed February 10, 2016, http://www
.pnas.org/content/107/38/16489.full.

2. Ed Diener and Martin E.P. Seligman, "Beyond Money,"
Psychological Science in the Public Interest, vol. 5, no. 1 (2004),
http://internal.psychology.illinois.edu/~ediener/Documents
/Diener-Seligman_2004.pdf.

Chapter 9: Engagement: Get in the Game!

1. Richard J. Foster, *Celebration of Discipline*, 25th ed. (New
York: HarperCollins, 2000), 128–130.

Chapter 11: Don't Try This Alone

1. Alistair Begg, Truth for Life.org,
2. Gary Collins, *Christian Coaching*, 2nd ed. (Colorado Springs:
NavPress, 2009), 23.

HALF|TIME
I N S T I T U T E™

The University for Your Second Half™

Founded by Bob Buford in 1998, the Halftime Institute provides successful marketplace men and women with teaching, coaching and connections they need to build a life defined by greater joy, Kingdom impact, and balance.

THE UNIVERSITY FOR YOUR SECOND HALF

The Halftime Institute offers a proven process to build on your success as you pursue significance. You and a group of peers begin an all-new chapter of spiritual, personal and professional purpose—maybe within the context of your current career . . . or perhaps not.

The Halftime Institute is a yearlong commitment that begins with a Launch Event: an intensive two days designed to dive deep into a systematic process, reflect and dream, and begin to design a road map of next steps.

Then, guided by your Halftime coach and surrounded by others who are on this same journey, you will address tough questions, craft a mission, rearrange commitments, and engage with those you love on a whole new level. We help you avoid many common mistakes of midlife transition.

 halftimeinstitute.org or call 855 2ND HALF